25 WALKS

In and Around
ABERDEEN

Turriff

A981

16●

A952

A90

River Ugie

17● Mintlaw
Maud

A950

Peterhead

14● Methlick

A948

River Ythan

15●

A90

13● Ellon

A920

A975

A920

12●

Newburgh

Oyne

River Urie

20●

A947

Inverurie

River Don

A90

19●

18● Kintore

Kemnay

21●

A96

11●

9● Dyce

8●

3●

Bridge of Don

Bankhead
Westhill

2●5

A944

Loch of
Skene

ABERDEEN

6●

4● 1●

10●

A93

River Dee

23●

22● Banchory

North

Sea

A957

24●

Cowie Water

25●
Stonehaven

A90

A92

Denie Water

N

Kilometres 0 ▰▰▰▰ 10
Miles 0 ▰▰▰ 5

25 WALKS

In and Around
ABERDEEN

Robert Smith

Revised by Peter Dawes and Alistair Mackenzie

Series Editor: Roger Smith

mercatpress

www.mercatpress.com

First published 1995
This edition published in 2004 by Mercat Press
Mercat Press Ltd., 10 Coates Crescent, Edinburgh EH3 7AL
© Mercat Press 2004
ISBN 184183 0097

Acknowledgements

The authors are grateful to Aberdeen City Council, Aberdeenshire
Council, Scottish Natural Heritage and the Upper Deeside Access Trust
for advice and information received during this latest revision.
Photographs are by Robert Smith, Peter Dawes, Alistair Mackenzie and
Scottish Natural Heritage.

All facts have been checked as far as possible but the authors and publisher
cannot be held responsible for any errors, however caused.

Cartography by MapSet Ltd., Newcastle upon Tyne
Reproduced by permission of Ordnance Survey on behalf of
The Controller of Her Majesty's Stationery Office
© Crown Copyright 100031557

Printed in Spain by Graficas Santamaría

CONTENTS

USEFUL INFORMATION

The length of each walk is given in kilometres and miles, but within the text, measurements are metric for simplicity. The walks are described in detail and are supported by accompanying maps, so you should not get lost, but if you want a back-up we recommend the Ordnance Survey 1:25,000 Explorer maps, which are on sale locally. Sheets 395, 396, 405 and 406 cover the area described in the book.

A reminder about countryside behaviour. If you have to open a farm gate, please ensure you close it behind you (if the gate is open it should be left that way); dogs must be kept on a lead in livestock areas and towns; and please be scrupulous about not dropping any litter. Routes described may or may not be rights of way. Farmers and land managers are usually friendly folk who work long hours to maintain the countryside we enjoy. When you meet, be helpful and friendly too!

Every care has been taken to make the descriptions and maps as accurate as possible, but the authors and publishers can accept no responsibility for errors, however caused. The countryside is always changing and there will inevitably be alterations to some aspects of these walks as time passes. The publishers would be happy to receive comments and suggested alterations for future editions.

Tourist Information

The Aberdeen and Grampian Tourist Board's website (*www.agtb.org*) contains a wealth of useful information. Tourist Information Centres are also great sources of information and help. Those within the book's area are Aberdeen (01224 288828), Inverurie (01807 580285), Banchory (01330 822000) and Stonehaven (01569 762806). The first two are open all year, the second two from Easter to October.

The public transport helpline number is 01224 212266.

For general information on walking in Scotland, visit the Walking Wild site at *www.walkingwild.com*

METRIC MEASUREMENTS

At the beginning of each walk, the distance is given in miles and kilometres. Within the text, all measurements are metric for simplicity (Ordnance Survey maps are also now all metric).

However, a conversion table might be still be useful.

The basic statistic to remember is that one kilometre is five-eighths of a mile. Half a mile is equivalent to 800 metres and a quarter-mile is 400 metres. Below that distance, yards and metres are little different in practical terms.

km	miles
1	0.625
1.6	1
2	1.25
3	1.875
3.2	2
4	2.5
4.8	3
5	3.125
6	3.75
6.4	4
7	4.375
8	5
9	5.625
10	6.25
16	10

INTRODUCTION

Aberdeen was once described by the poet Iain Crichton Smith as "a town of pure crystal". He loved its "brilliant streets" and the sight of mica glittering on its white stone. It is a city of granite and roses – it regularly wins prizes in the Britain in Bloom competition.

Aberdeen has been called the Silver City with the Golden Sands, so the book takes you to the seaside to walk the Prom, to wander round the Bay of Nigg to Girdleness Lighthouse and the old Torry Battery, and to see the busy harbour, where oil vessels have taken the place of the fishing trawlers.

Then you can follow the old Deeside railway line – on foot. The route along the "subbie line" passes through some lovely scenery. There is another kind of charm in Old Aberdeen, with King's College and its chapel, the old Town House, St Machar's Cathedral and the path by the River Don to the ancient Brig o' Balgownie.

These are some of the walks in Aberdeen. Others are outside the city boundary, but are within easy reach. Public transport details are given in the text. The walks range from Deeside to Donside, into Buchan, south to the Mearns, and along the coast to the Sands of Forvie.

You'll find plenty of variety – crossing the Braes o' Gight to the ruins of brooding Gight Castle, walking in the stately grounds of Haddo House, watching the wonderful wildlife at Forvie, climbing an Observatory overlooking an abandoned racecourse, or following the former Formartine and Buchan railway line, now a walkway. That's a taste of what the book offers, and there is much more.

The walks range from 5km (3 miles) to 13km (8 miles) and most are ideal for families. Advice on what to wear, toilets and transport, refreshments and opening hours can be found in the information panels. Whether walking in the Granite City itself or in its fine countryside, this book will help to make it a rewarding experience.

This new edition has been thoroughly revised and updated and new walks included. Details are believed to be correct as at autumn 2004.

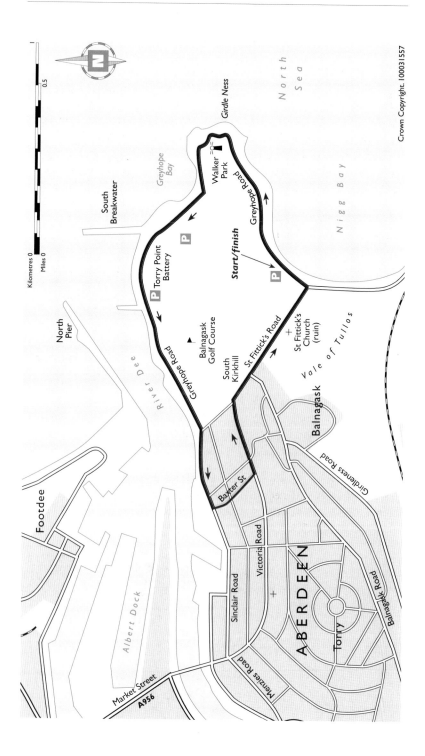

Crown Copyright. 100031557

BAY OF NIGG

The townsfolk of Aberdeen once flocked to the Bay of Nigg to cure their ills at a "miracle" well, a superstitious practice that the City Fathers tried to stop. More recently, in pre-war years, people looked after their health in a different way – they turned the Bay into the city's playground, a picnicker's paradise where they could breathe in the sea air.

Nowadays, the Bay is largely deserted. This is where your walk starts, taking in three bays that mark the approach to this bustling oil port. It starts at a car park on the edge of the shore, but if you travel to Nigg by bus you can set out from the Balnagask golf course, a few hundred metres away. There is a bus stop outside the clubhouse.

From the car park, the road south goes along the cliffs to Cove, but your route lies in the opposite direction, towards Girdleness Lighthouse. Look for granite steps in a walled area on the left. They lead to Torry's first and only public park – the Walker Park, where the lighthouse keepers grazed their cattle more than a century and a half ago.

Near here, you will come upon a different kind of cow or, as the local dialect has it, a "coo" – the Torry Coo. This was the name given to the Girdleness foghorn, whose melancholy bellow

INFORMATION

Distance: 4km (2.5 miles) circular.

Start and finish: Bay of Nigg. From Market Street, cross Victoria Bridge to Torry. Follow Victoria Road turning right into St Fittick's Road which leads to the Bay of Nigg. Parking area at the Bay.

Terrain: Easy walking. Pavements and paths all the way. No special footwear needed.

Refreshments: Cafes and shops in Torry.

Public transport: Good bus service from city centre.

Aberdeen harbour

The Torry Coo

could be heard clear across the city on a foggy night. It stands on the rocks below the 131ft (39m) lighthouse which was built in 1832-33 by Robert Stevenson, grandfather of Robert Louis Stevenson. Sadly, the "coo" has now been silenced and the lighthouse has been automated.

The road goes through a series of bends and as it straightens out you are looking down on a small but historic inlet called Greyhope Bay. This was where a whaler called the *Oscar* went down in 1813, with the loss of 55 lives. Only two men survived. It was after this disaster that a call went out for a lighthouse, but 20 years passed before it was built.

The long finger of the South Breakwater is on your right. The road swings round to hug the line of the navigation channel and on your left is the Torry Point Battery, with the date 1861 inscribed over the arched entrance. It was originally armed with 60-pounder guns, but the Battery has rarely fired a shot in anger. It banged away at two unidentified ships in 1941 but they turned out to be friendly.

Near the Battery, above Greyhope Road, there is a car park where motorists come to sit and enjoy an incomparable view of Aberdeen and its sea-front: the busy harbour, the wide sweep of Aberdeen Bay and the spires and steeples that reach up from the grey granite heart of the city. People think of the Bay as a two-mile crescent of sand between the Dee and the Don but, in fact, from Girdle Ness to the sands of Forvie in the north, Aberdeen Bay is 13 miles (21km) wide – as one report on Scotland's coastline put it, "one of the longest stretches of beach and dune coastline in Highland Scotland".

Across the channel, cormorants preen themselves on the wall of the North Pier, watching the parade of fishing boats and giant oil ships moving up the channel. Old men and young boys once sat on the pier and fished for saithe, fish which fed on the sewer outlets. There is a link with this in an ugly brick obelisk on the pier known as Scarty's Monument. Scarty was a harbour pilot, William Smith, who was a bit of a character, and his "monument" is, in fact, a ventilator shaft for one of the sewers.

Leaving the Torry Battery and continuing down Greyhope Road until you reach Campbell's pub on the corner, the way straight ahead is blocked by a fence and a gate carrying the sign, "Total E+P UK. PLC. No unauthorised entry." Once you could walk down Torry Quay, for this world of oil and big business was originally the fishing community of Old Torry, wiped out when the oilmen came.

Turn left up Sinclair Road and then left up Baxter Street, passing some old houses, one bearing the date 1891. Turn left again at the top of Baxter Street, which will take you on to Victoria Road. Here, on the left, you pass the Marine Laboratory run by the Fisheries Research Services.

Torry Battery

Balnagask golf course stands at the junction of Victoria Road and St Fittick's Road. The last lap of your walk, however, is down St Fittick's Road to the car park at the Bay of Nigg. Here, you are on the edge of a little valley called the Vale of Tullos, which is on your right. Today, the Vale has been largely buried by housing development.

Over on the grassland on the right is the ruined St Fittick's Church with a leper's squint, an ancient belfry and a walled graveyard full of lurching tombstones. In one corner of the old kirkyard is the watchhouse used early last century during the time of the bodysnatchers. Access to the kirkyard is possible by obtaining a key at the Starter's Hut near the Balnagask golf clubhouse.

St Fittick's Well was in this area. It was here, on the first Sunday of the year, that people came to drink the "miracle" waters.

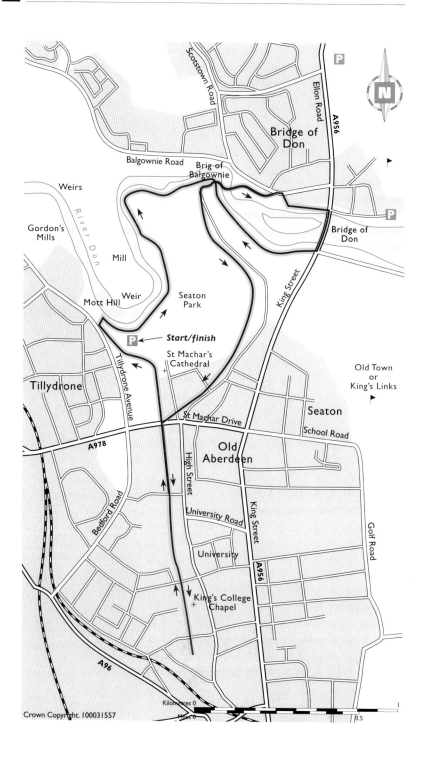

Scotstown Road

Ellon Road

A956

P

N

Bridge of
Don

Balgownie Road   Brig of
Balgownie

Weirs

River Don

Gordon's
Mills

P

Bridge of
Don

Mill

King Street

Weir

Mott Hill

Seaton
Park

P   ← *Start/finish*

St Machar's
Cathedral

Old Town
or
King's Links

Tillydrone

Tillydrone Avenue

Seaton

St Machar Drive

School Road

A978

Old
Aberdeen

High Street

Bedford Road

University Road

King Street

University

A956

Golf Road

King's College
Chapel

A96

Kilometres 0

Miles 0

0.5

AULTON AND SEATON

Enjoy a quiet start to this walk by taking a look round the park. The name "Seaton" means "peaceful retreat", and that is what it is. It was less peaceful in the 19th century when it was used as a racecourse. The last race was run in 1928. Now you can stroll in its sheltered rose gardens, take the youngsters to the railway wagons and the brake van in the adventure playground, or walk by the river.

Swans, mallards and moorhens can be seen on the grassy flats of the River Don, whose dark waters surge away towards the old Brig o' Balgownie. The path downriver rises high above the tree-lined gorge of Balgownie. On the right of the path is the students' residence at Hillhead of Seaton.

When you leave Seaton Park, the alternative route turns right into Don Street. Otherwise, turn left and the first house on your left is the Chapter House (it is, incidentally, misnamed), which has the initials GC and BH and the date 1655 over an arched pend with a coat of arms. GC was George Cruickshank, who built the house, and BH was his wife, Barbara Hervie.

Nearby is the Balgownie Mission Hall, and where the cobbled road turns right, another group of houses adds to the old-world charm of this corner by the Don. The famous Brig o' Balgownie, built in the late 13th and early 14th centuries, completes

INFORMATION

Distance: 5km (3miles) circular.

Start and finish: Car park at Seaton Park in far left hand corner.

Terrain: Good walking, but path from Seaton Park to the Brig o' Balgownie can be muddy in wet weather. Alternative route by Don Street advisable for unfit or elderly people. Strong footwear recommended.

Public transport: Good bus service from the city centre.

Refreshments: Excellent restaurant in Visitor's Centre at King's College. There is also a café in the High Street used by students.

Toilets: In Seaton Park.

Opening hours: King's College, St Machar's Cathedral: open daily 0900–1700; Cruickshank Botanic Garden: open all year Mon–Fri 0900–1630, May–Sep. Sat–Sun 1400–1700.

Brig of Balgownie

the picture. The brig has been rightly described as "one of the most hauntingly beautiful Gothic survivals in Scotland".

Beyond the brig is the Cot Town of Balgownie, whose ancient red-tiled cottages were restored by a private developer. The house nearest the brig, built about 1600, was originally known as the Black Nook Alehouse. It took its name from the Black Nook Port, a dark pool to the west of the bridge, where evil spirits are said to have lured passers-by to their deaths.

The centuries slipped away and the ancient bridge settled into its niche in the history books, while a new bridge was built over the Don. This was completed in 1830 at a cost of £16,000, and it in turn was replaced by a newer, wider bridge in 1959. To get to the Bridge of Don, cross the Old Brig and turn right down steps to the river bank and a path taking you to the north end of the new bridge. Cross over the bridge and turn immediately right on a path taking you back towards the Old Brig. There are seats and an information board on this path and good views of the pointed arch of the Old Brig.

When you reach the roadway again, turn left up Don Street, which was once known as Seatongate, the "gait" or way to Seaton. Its picturesque houses also have their stories – no. 78, for instance, carries the name Bishop's Port, although the Bishop's Port or East Port was actually on the other side of the street.

In Clark's Lane, adjoining the west gable of the Bishop's Port, are four single-storey cottages with red-tiled roofs and roses round the doors. The Dower House is at no. 49, built on the side of the Cathedral treasurer's house, and Bede House, built in 1676, is at nos. 20 and 22. This old building, which has a projecting tower and a corbelled stair turret, is now let to municipal tenants and is known as Bede House Court.

Leaving Don Street, you cross St Machar Drive to the High Street and into the Aulton, where history is on your heels at almost every corner. Enter the High Street along the side of the Town House, in front of which stands the restored Mercat Cross. The distance between the two market crosses of New Aberdeen and Old Aberdeen was once said to be a "large Scottish mile". The route followed the old highway to the north, up the Gallowgate to Mounthooly and over the Spital Brae to College Bounds and the High Street. Today, that "Scottish mile" represents a giant step into the past.

King's College

If King's College crowns one end of High Street, the old Town House crowns the other. This late 18th-century Georgian building, three storeys high, has a clock tower topped by a cupola. Over the entrance is the burgh coat of arms dated 1721. Barely noticeable across the road from the Town House is Market Lane, a link with the old Aulton Fair, or St Luke's Fair. Nearby, Baillie Place recalls the former burgh status of Old Aberdeen. Much of the fascination of the Aulton lies in exploring its wynds, courts and closes.

Soon you come on the left to a striking gateway to both Old and New King's Colleges and to the Old Brewery. Beer from the Old Brewery, which is now a University department, once went out from the Aulton to Balmoral Castle. The name is also perpetuated in nearby Brewery Lane.

Across the grounds on the left is Elphinstone Hall, part of the complex of buildings that make up "King's" today. The whole is dominated by the magnificent Crown Tower above the Chapel. On the lawn beneath it is the bronze and marble monument to William Elphinstone, Bishop of Aberdeen, who founded King's College in 1498.

New King's Arch

From the High Street, where a sign points the way to the King's College Conference and Visitor's

Centre, you can make your way through the quadrangle to the restaurant and souvenir shop that form part of the centre. Across the road, no.1 High Street has a door lintel carrying the name "College Place". See if you can guess the meaning of the curious sign – a gilt sun – on the wall. In fact, in the 18th century, fire insurance companies kept their own fire brigades. And to the houses which were insured with them, they fixed a fire mark – a thin metal plate showing the company's sign and sometimes the number of the policy. Thus the fire brigade would put its best foot forward when they knew that the burning property was insured by their company.

Further along on the same side, two curious minarets adorn the huge Powis Lodge gate at the entrance to the Crombie Hall of Residence. The minarets were erected by John Leslie, a young laird of Powis, as a tribute to Lord Byron.

This is the turning point of the walk and you must retrace your steps along High Street, probably seeing lots of little details you missed previously. Before you leave the High Street and cross to the Chanonry, take a look at the house round the corner at 60 St Machar Drive, Cluny's Port. The St Machar's Cathedral precincts were enclosed by four ports or gateways and Cluny's Port, originally called Chanonry Port, was the south gateway. It was the gatehouse to Cluny's Gardens, now the Cruickshank Botanical Garden, on the other side of St Machar Drive. It is well worth a visit.

The Chanonry runs its stately tree-lined way to St Machar's Cathedral. Its large dignified houses mostly belong to the 18th or early 19th centuries. In sharp contrast is no. 9. This is Mitchell's Hospital, originally built in 1801 "to clothe and maintain five widows and five unmarried daughters of Merchant and Trade Burgesses of Old Aberdeen." Note the sundial in the court.

Number 13, almost opposite the main gateway of the Cathedral, is Chanonry Lodge, the home of the Principal of the University. Here, the Chanonry takes a right-angle turn and runs down to Don Street. Number 20 is Chaplain's Court, whose moulded pend arch is surmounted with the arms of Bishop Gavin Dunbar who built the original Chaplain's Court in 1519.

St Machar's Cathedral

The great fortified church of St Machar's Cathedral, dating back to the 14th century, rises over the Chanonry, its twin spires known to every Aberdonian and to thousands of visitors. In its graveyard lie the great and the good – and some perhaps not quite so good. Margery Laing is among them. Margery, whose single name was May Gray, was nursemaid to Lord Byron. It is said that when he was a young man she seduced him and was sacked, and sent home from England in disgrace.

From the Cathedral, at the entrance to Seaton Park, your route lies up Tillydrone Road. This "cassied" road, which was the old route to the north, takes you to Benholm's Lodging, better known to Aberdonians as the Wallace Tower, although it had no connection with the Scots hero. In 1963, it was taken down from its site in the Netherkirkgate and rebuilt stone by stone on Tillydrone Hill. The grassy mound at the summit of the hill is the Motte of Tillydrone, the site of a 12th century fort commanding a ford across the River Don.

Go past the Wallace Tower to a wall, on the far side of which a marker post points you on a path down to the river bank and back into Seaton Park, leaving behind you the sights and sounds of an ancient community whose beauty will linger long in your mind.

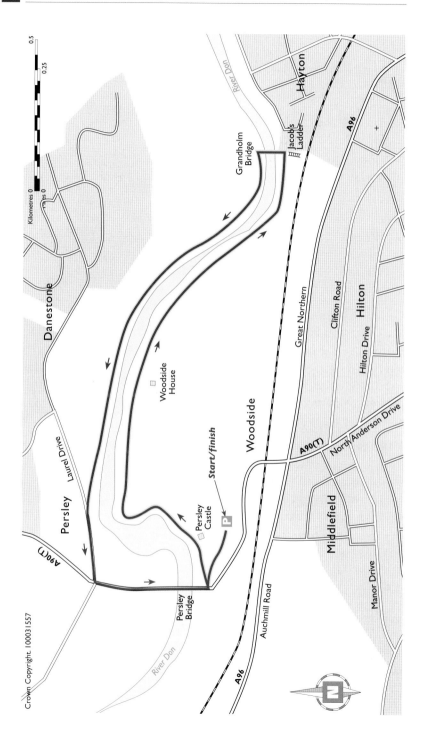

Crown Copyright. 100031557

Kilometres 0 0.25 0.5

Miles 0

River Don

Danestone

Persley

Laurel Drive

A90(T)

Persley Bridge

River Don

A96

Auchmill Road

Woodside House

Persley Castle

Start/finish

P

Woodside

A90(T)

North Anderson Drive

Middlefield

Manor Drive

Grandholm Bridge

Jacob's Ladder

Hayton

A96

Great Northern

Clifton Road

Hilton Drive

Hilton

PERSLEY AND GRANDHOLM

A ladder to heaven awaits the walker on the Woodside nature trail in Aberdeen. The trail links two well-known bridges – Persley and Grandholm – and runs along the banks of the River Don, whose mighty waters were once harnessed for the mills that operated in the Grandholm area.

From the car park, have a look at the interesting walled garden which was restored and reopened in 1997 as part of the STUC centenary. The workers' memorial inside is particularly appropriate in view of the huge amount of industry which once operated down the banks of the river.

On leaving the garden, turn immediately right on a red ash path, and when it reaches the road, turn sharp right again through a gate on a track heading for the river. At a ruined house with arched windows, go straight on to have a look at a large imposing building which was at one time known locally as Persley Castle.

Half hidden in the trees high above the Don, its castellated structure speaks of a romantic past, but there was no spirit of romance when this fort-like building was erected. It also became known as the Barracks, for it was built to house children who were used as sweated labour for calico printing. It was built at the beginning of the 19th century, later became a sawmill, and is now a care home for the elderly.

INFORMATION

Distance: 4km (2.5 miles) circular.

Start and finish: Persley walled garden car park. From the roundabout at the junction of Anderson Drive and Great Northern Road, go down Mugiemoss Road and turn right into Hutcheon Low Drive. Car park on left.

Terrain: The tracks and footpaths vary on the walk; some sections require a certain amount of care. No special footwear is required.

Refreshments and toilets: Tesco Extra store, Laurel Drive.

Public transport: Good bus service from the city centre.

Persley Castle

The track to the Barracks is a dead end, so retrace your steps to the ruined house which was the gate-house and is our "gateway" to Grandholm. Go down steps at the side of the building onto a narrow path dropping steeply to the riverside. Running parallel to the riverside path is the dried-up channel of the Upper Mill Lade, which brought water to the machinery of Woodside Works, where cotton manufacture was introduced to Aberdeen in 1779. By 1822, more than 3000 people were employed there. It closed in 1851.

Broken walls, sluice gates, mill lades... Nature softens these relics of the mills whose lifeblood came from the Don. At one grassy clearing, there are giant links with the old cotton factory at Woodside. Two huge flywheels, supported by stanchions, dominate this peaceful rural scene. The wheels, water-powered by the mill lade, turned the factory machinery. An even bigger 75-ton wheel, built for Grandholm Mills, was sent to the Royal Scottish Museum.

Old mill flywheels from Grandholm Works

As you head along the trail, past some ruins, you can see Grandholm Bridge in the distance. At its south end is Jacob's Ladder, its narrow steps rising up to Don Terrace. Its name was inspired by the Old Testament story of how Jacob saw in a dream a ladder reaching up to heaven. Maybe it had its own special meaning for the thousands of Grandholm workers who struggled up its 66 steps at the end of a hard day's work to reach their "heaven on earth" – their homes in the villages of Cottown, Tanfield, and Printfield, which were later combined to form the burgh of Woodside. Today, there are two Jacob's Ladders. The old "ladder" is closed off and overgrown. The modern "ladder", still in use, has 97 steps, but they are 4m wide and go up in stages, making it much easier to ascend.

Cross the bridge, and on your right above the rooftops of a new housing estate you should spot the square tower, all that remains of Grandholm

Mills, which belonged to J & J Crombie Ltd. The Crombies, whose name is known throughout the world for cloth, had a mill at Cothal, or Little Fintray, and took over Grandholm in 1859. One feature of the mill was Grandholm Big Wheel, the biggest water wheel in the world, which was 8m in diameter, 6m wide, and used 115,000 cubic feet of water per minute. It was demolished in 1905. There are plans to house a heritage centre in the tower which will tell the story of the mill.

From the bridge, turn upriver through a gap in the wall. The path rises and falls in places, with side tracks, mostly used by fishermen, branching off to the river. Take the right-hand path – the "high" road – which you'll find easier. For part of the way, the path sticks closely to a fence, and where the fence ends there is a steep, sandy drop to a bigger track. It is difficult and slippery, but it can be avoided by going a little left and following an easier route.

Persley Bridge and the River Don

Once on the main track, you will see a lade on your right and a path crossing it. This takes you out on to the road near Tesco, but to complete the nature trail carry straight on, following the river until you come to the sluice gates which controlled the lade to Grandholm Mills. From here, climb up to a side road below Tesco, turn left, and walk along to Persley Bridge. Cross the bridge on the left-hand pavement and keep an eye open for a stone at the end of the bridge marked '49ABD'. This is a March Stone, one of 67 which mark the Freedom Lands of Aberdeen, granted to the town by Robert the Bruce in the 14th century. Once over the bridge, turn left on the red ash path back to the car park.

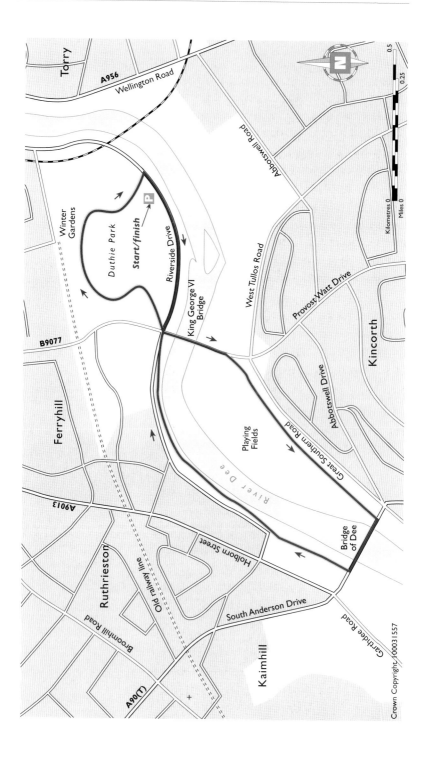

THE DEE AND DUTHIE PARK

From the car park and the boating pond, which comes alive in the summer holidays with children enjoying the boats for hire, walk along the park road running parallel to Riverside Drive towards the West Gate. High above, a tall red granite obelisk rears its stately head. It was erected in honour of Sir James McGrigor, Director General of the Army Medical Department in the Peninsular War. Look out too for an old ivy-covered well. This is the Fountainhall Well, which three centuries ago played an important role in the city's water supply. It was taken from its original site and rebuilt at Duthie Park in 1903.

From the West Gate, cross Riverside Drive to the King George VI Bridge, which was opened in 1941 and was intended to take traffic away from the Bridge of Dee. However, over half a century later while the planners argue about yet another bridge, cars and lorries are still jamming its 16th century predecessor.

The George VI Bridge was opened by Queen Elizabeth, later the Queen Mother, who had the pawky

INFORMATION

Distance: 4km (2.5 miles) circular.

Start and finish: Duthie car park. Enter by the east gate off Riverside Drive.

Terrain: Footpaths and pavements. No special footwear needed.

Refreshments: Restaurant in Duthie Park. Open 09.00–17.00 in summer, 10.00–16.00 in winter.

Toilets: In Duthie Park.

Monument to Sir James McGrigor

Lord Provost Sir Tommy Mitchell at her side. Tommy forgot his lines and said to the Queen in an audible whisper, "I'm afraid of making a hash of this!" Further downstream is another royal bridge, the Queen Elizabeth Bridge, opened in 1983.

Cross the bridge by the west pavement and make your way along Great Southern Road, passing attractive flower beds with Inverdee playing fields on your right. The last building before the Bridge of Dee is a hotel called The Gillies' Lair. Immediately before the bridge, cross the road to the west side in order to check the time – not on your watch, but on a sundial. You'll find it on steps next to the bridge leading down into a pleasant garden. On it you can see the date 1719 and a curious set of initials – AWMROBW. These are the initials of Alexander Watson, who was elected Master of Bridge Works (MROBW) in 1718, holding the office for a year.

The old Bridge of Dee

The sundial was put on the bridge when repairs were carried out in 1719, but for a long time it was useless, for the iron gnomon, the arm which projects the shadow onto the sundial, disappeared last century. It was eventually replaced. The roar of traffic rises above the bridge but, whatever the sundial shows, time really stands still in this quiet little garden. Once the site of a coachhouse, the garden sits on the path of the Causey Mounth, the old route south from Aberdeen.

History has left its mark on the old brig. It bears a tremendous collection of coats of arms and commemorative inscriptions, the oldest going back to 1520. One stone carries the inscription "Gavin Dunbar caused me to be built over the River Dee, AD1525." Gavin Dunbar was the Bishop who saw the bridge through to its final completion in 1527. Some of the crests can be seen from the garden, others from the north bank of the river.

Climb the steps past the sundial and walk to the north end of the bridge. Keeping one eye on the traffic, cross the road and go down a footpath that follows the Dee on its way to the sea. From the riverside here, you can see the bridge's seven semi-circular ribbed arches. It has been described as Aberdeen's finest single monument of the Middle Ages. At one time, it had a chapel for wayfarers and a great port or gateway.

Across the river, the housing estate of Kincorth climbs up the hill of Kincorth, some of its streets carrying names like Covenanters' Row and Faulds' Gate. They mark a site called Covenanters' Faulds, where the campfires of the covenanting army blazed on the eve of the Battle of the Bridge of Dee in 1639:

> Upon the 18th day of June,
> A dreary day to see,
> The southern lords did pitch their camp
> Just at the Bridge of Dee.

In the spring, the grassy banks on the north side of the river are bright with daffodils, stretching away in a golden carpet towards the river mouth. Up on your left is Riverside Drive, planned in 1875 as a broad carriage drive next to the river. The river itself curves through a historic area where Ruadri, a Celtic Mormaer of Mar, had a motte and bailey stronghold overlooking the ford where travellers crossed the Dee. Ruthrieston (Ruddreistoun) once had an annual fair, but now the old hamlet has vanished into the granite maw of the city. There is still a link with the past in an old pack-bridge built in 1693-94 to span the Ruthrieston Burn. It was built without parapets so that pack-horses could get over it without difficulty.

The old packhorse bridge

Like the Bridge of Dee, it is decorated with heraldic panels and inscriptions. One panel was the cause of a row between the Provost and the City Fathers. Provost Robert Cruickshank, whose daughter married Alexander Watson, the Master of Works at the Bridge of Dee, annoyed the magistrates by putting his coat of arms on the bridge without permission. When he was no longer Provost, they took down the stone, cut another inscription on the reverse side, and stuck it back on the bridge. Seven years later, the stone was restored to its original position.

The pack-bridge was shifted 30 metres to the east in 1923 and rebuilt with parapets, which destroyed its original character. It is not much of a brig but when you cross it you can pause and remind yourself that you are standing on centuries of Aberdeen history.

So it is over the pack bridge and down the river path, past the fisherman's bothy to reach the King George VI Bridge again. At the roundabout, cross to the west gate of Duthie Park, through which you go to circle the park. Take the middle road from the gate to a pond spanned by a large bridge. There are in fact two linked ponds where ducks and moorhens paddle about, snooze on the islands, or come ashore for titbits. There are toilets just beyond the top pond. Go left from here and ahead you will see the small red and grey temperance fountain. "Thou gavest them water for their thirst" says the inscription, but the water has dried up. From the fountain, go left up a grassy space between trees and turn right at the war memorial. In front of you is the Mound.

This knoll, which is a blaze of roses in bloom in summer, was originally intended to take the largest flagpole in the north of Scotland. That novel idea never came off, and so the next plan was to put William Wallace's statue on top of it. Wallace, however, landed up on Union Terrace.

Follow the road at the foot of the Mound until you come to the famous Winter Gardens, now called the David Welch Winter Gardens. With a wealth of tropical plants, sculptures, curios and antiquities, the gardens are immensely popular with both visitors and local people. The exhibits range from Kelly's cats, which once decorated the south side of Union Bridge, to the wheelbarrow used when Duthie Park's first turf was cut in August 1881.

From the Winter Gardens, you look across the parkland to a splendid Victorian bandstand, a silent monument to the days of the brass bands. Next to the gardens is the restaurant; beyond it, take a road which circles the park down past a monument dedicated to Elizabeth Crombie Duthie who gifted the park to the city. This will lead you nicely back to the car park and the exit to Riverside Drive.

The colourful Winter Gardens

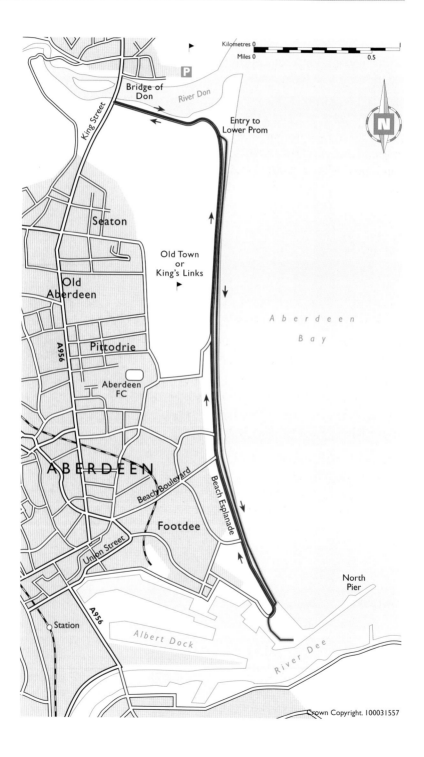

THE PROM

Aberdeen's beach promenade runs for 3km (two miles) along the sea front, linking the Rivers Dee and Don. A walk on the Prom is popular with Aberdeen folk and for some people it is a trip down memory lane, back to the long-lost days when they listened to the "oompa" bands on the Links, laughed at Harry Gordon in the Pavilion, and sat on deckchairs on the sands.

The starting point of the walk is the old fishing village of Fittie or Futty, a name that last century was corruptly anglicised to Footdee. Two hundred years ago it was a row of thatched cottages, but in 1808-9 it was rebuilt near the North Pier. The North and South Squares came first, followed by the Middle Row and Pilot's Square.

Before setting out it is worth exploring the old "fisher toun". Look for the Tower of Babylon, a tall building rising above a row of cottages. No one is quite sure how it got its name. Babylon, of course, was a place of depravity, but the Fittie fishers would shy away from such things.

Your route is along the sea-front by the high road – the Beach Esplanade, or upper Prom – and back by the lower promenade. To the left lie the spires and tower blocks of the city, while to the right is the great sprawl of Aberdeen Bay. Beyond the fence on the opposite side of the road are all that remains of Aberdeen's once flourishing ship-building industry.

INFORMATION

Distance: 6 km (4 miles) circular.

Start and finish: Footdee (Fittie). Main approach from Union Street by car is by King Street, East North Street, and Beach Boulevard. Parking at Fittie and on Esplanade.

Terrain: Pavements and tarmac paths. No special footwear needed.

Refreshments: There are restaurants, cafes and shops on the Promenade.

Toilets: At both ends of the walk at Fittie and the Bridge of Don. Also on the Lower Promenade opposite the Boulevard.

Public transport: Good bus service from the city centre.

Entertainment: Codona's Amusement Park, the Beach Ballroom, the Beach Leisure Centre with swimming, ice-skating and sports facilities, the Links golf course and golf driving range.

Aberdeen Beach
seen from Fittie

A picturesque corner of Fittie

Less than half a mile from Fittie is the Prom's busiest section, a line of cafes, ice cream shops and an amusement arcade. Here, too, was Inversnecky, the mythical home of Harry Gordon, who played to packed houses in the Beach Pavilion. A Continental Cafe stands on the site now and the only reminders of the Laird of Inversnecky's reign are a cafe called Inversnecky and another called the Pavilion. Behind the shops is Codona's Amusement Park, with its dodgem cars, stalls and scenic railway.

Where the Beach Boulevard runs up towards the city centre, two old tramlines can be seen cutting through the Queen's Links. The "trammies" once came rattling down this track from the Castlegate. Nearby there was a magnificent bandstand where concerts were held – it cost you two old pennies for a seat. Farther back is the Broad Hill, once known as Cunningar Hill, a name that means 'rabbity'. It is a mere 94 ft (30m) in height, but you get a nice view from the top.

On the Prom, a fenced-in seating area marks the site of the Beach Shelter, which was topped by a superb clock. The City Fathers in their wisdom – and to the annoyance of many Aberdonians – allowed it to deteriorate and finally demolished it.

As you walk along the Prom, you will see adjoining the Beach Ballroom two comparatively new leisure centres, including a swimming pool and an ice rink. After that, the King's Links stretch away to the east, most of it given over to an 18-hole golf course. Across the Links is Gallowhill, where a familiar landmark – the city's old gasometer – stood until recently, and near it is Aberdeen FC's ground at Pittodrie.

People were kicking a ball on the Links long before the Dons appeared on the scene. James Gordon, Parson of Rothiemay, said football was played on "the fair plaine called the Queen's Lynks in 1661", along with "goffe, bowling and archerie".

"Here likewayse", said the Parson, "they walk for

their health". So encouraged, step along the Prom towards the mouth of the Don. On the left, as you walk, you get a good view over the city.

The road swings to the left as you reach the estuary and runs parallel to the river as far as King Street and the Bridge of Don. Upstream, the river comes tumbling under the ancient Brig o' Balgownie (see Walk 2) before reaching the Don Bridge, built in 1831 at a cost of about £17,000. The river bank here is now a local nature reserve and you will see a bird-watching hide on the edge of the grass area.

The Bridge of Don at Donmouth

In the 1960s, erosion was so bad at the beach that it was feared that it would destroy the unprotected dunes, so that the Promenade would have to be abandoned and the invading spring tides would lap the city. Such a disaster was avoided by laying out a system of groynes along the seafront. A pre-cast coping with promenade walk was also laid down halfway up the dunes. Today, that "promenade walk" – the lower Prom – is where hundreds of people stroll by the sea.

When you retrace your steps from the Bridge of Don look for an opening taking you down onto the Prom. It can be seen where the road swings right towards Fittie. There are a number of shelters along the lower Prom and steps down to the sand all the way to Fittie.

The ghosts of yesteryear haunt the area near the site of the old Beach Baths. Here were bathing huts and ice-cream stalls, pierrot shows and brass bands – and Aberdeen's famous golden sands, buried under a mountain of deckchairs. Now people sit in their cars and watch the sea or "promenade" along the sea-front.

On the last leg of the walk you can see the North Pier poking its finger out to sea and in the distance the silhouette of the Torry Battery on Balnagask. Then you are back at Fittie, having completed your Walk on the Prom.

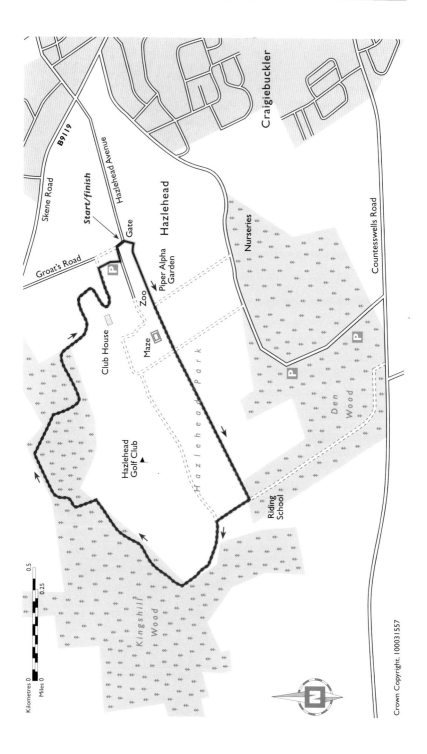

HAZLEHEAD

W hen Aberdeen Town Council bought the 852-acre estate of Hazlehead in 1920, a letter to the local paper criticised the move and complained that people were "already under a burden of taxation unprecedented in the history of this country". The cost was just £40,000.

Eighty years later, this walk shows you what Aberdonians got for their money. The starting point is the car park at the junction of Groats Road and Hazlehead Avenue. Directly opposite is the entrance to the park, beside a small Tudor-style cottage. There are steps down to the cottage and you can enter the park this way or by the main gate.

When you enter the park, ignore for the moment the path on the right, which leads to a big red-roofed shelter. Instead, follow the path ahead of you. It curves round past a row of beech trees and takes you to the park's heather garden. Heather is always regarded as Scotland's own special plant, but there are varieties in the garden from as far afield as Spain and Italy. You'll also see some lucky white heather there!

From the heather garden, you can cut through to the path from the gate. Almost adjacent to the shelter is the entrance to Hazlehead's miniature zoo, where there is a free-flying aviary, a large aquarium, rabbits, donkeys, chipmunks, llamas, goats and several breeds of ducks. Children will love it.

INFORMATION

Distance: 6km (3.5 miles) circular.

Start and finish: Car park at entrance to Hazlehead Park, another near golf club house.

Terrain: Good walking, although the track in the woodland section of the route can be muddy in wet weather.

Refreshments: Café in Hazlehead Park, open Apr.-Sept.

Public transport: Good bus service from the city centre to Hazlehead roundabout, then walk up Hazlehead Avenue.

Toilets: In the park.

Hazlehead Park

Leaving the zoo, go back to the heather garden and turn right – the park restaurant can be seen up ahead. The restaurant, with its Continental-style patio, pool and fountain, was built in 1960.

One of the Bruce cairns

When Aberdeen Town Council bought the estate in 1920, they were in a sense buying back their own land, for Hazlehead was part of the vast territory known as the Freedom Lands, gifted to the town by Robert the Bruce in 1319. The link with Bruce is recalled in a series of cairns near the restaurant. Each has a historical scene carved on it – Bruce at Bannockburn, Bruce and the Spider, and Bruce presenting the Freedom Lands to the citizens of Aberdeen.

The cairns are just beyond the restaurant and a little further on is the maze. People have been getting lost behind its towering privet hedges since 1935, when it was given to the city by Sir Henry Alexander, a former Lord Provost. Don't worry, there's a watcher there to guide you if you can't find your way out. The maze is open April to September.

Directly opposite the maze, across the main path through the main park, is the North Sea Memorial Garden, recalling the tragic day in July 1988, when 167 men died on the Piper Alpha platform 208km offshore in the North Sea. Only 61 men were rescued. The sculpted figures of three oil-men stand out starkly on top of the memorial in the centre of the garden.

Piper Alpha monument

Next to the Piper Alpha garden is another rose garden – the Queen Mother Rose Garden, commemorating the royal lady's 80th birthday.

What appears to be a trio of standing stones are grouped together in one of the gardens. In fact, these giant stone slabs were intended to be sculpted into granite lions for the King George VI Bridge over the River Dee, which was opened in 1941. The plan was dropped and in 1970 they were taken to Hazlehead and given the name Hazlehenge.

Near the western boundary of the park, where you go through a gate, cross a minor road, and continue on a tarmacadam track stretching ahead between the fairways of Hazlehead golf course. As you get near the top of the road, you pass a track going left to Hayfield riding school.

A little way ahead is a T-junction. Turn right and you come to another junction marked by a triangle of grass with a few trees on it. You'll find a drinking fountain here and also a seat where you can take a breather and watch the golfers driving down the 12th hole. Go left at the junction and follow the path as it runs parallel with the 12th hole towards a green shelter in the distance. Bear left again at the shelter. The track swings left, but your route is by a narrower track going off to the right and into the woods.

You come eventually to a corner where the trees open out and you are running parallel with another track to your left, the two tracks being separated by an "island" of trees. Note the dry-stane dykes – they were built at least a century ago. Behind them is an area of parkland where young trees have been planted and paths laid out.

From the track, you get an interesting view over the city, including the Woodend Hospital clock tower and the communication mast on Anderson Drive. The fairways are in front of you again and you turn sharp left, passing the 18th tee. Look down the fairway and you will see the "19th hole" – Hazlehead Golf Club.

The track wanders past Hazlehead Academy playing fields and ends up behind the clubhouse. Go round it and follow the road back to the car park opposite the entrance to Hazlehead.

Alternatively, go left down a tree-lined path which passes the entrance to an old caravan site. When you reach Groats Road, turn right and the car park is a short distance ahead.

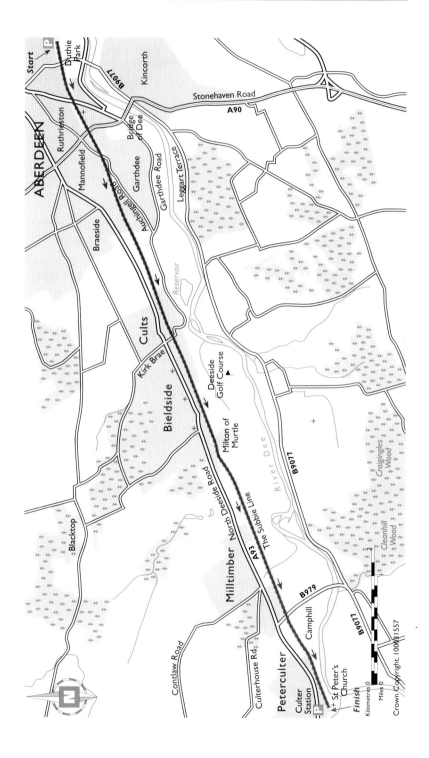

Crown Copyright. 100031557

THE SUBBIE LINE

The Greek goddess of health, Hygeia, gives you a send-off when you walk the old Deeside railway line from Aberdeen's Duthie Park. She stands on top of a tall Corinthian column erected in 1898 in memory of Elizabeth Crombie Duthie, who gifted the land to the city to be used as a public park.

The park itself was opened in 1883. Thirty years earlier, the Duchess of Kent became the Deeside line's first Royal patron when she travelled by train from Banchory to Ferryhill Station. Queen Victoria followed two days later.

Hygeia's statue is only a short distance from the car park at the Polmuir Road entrance. Here, a few stone steps take you on to the Royal line ready for a healthy tramp to Culter, which was the terminus of the old Deeside suburban train service. On the left as you walk are the Winter Gardens, containing a wealth of tropical plants, sculptures and curios, while on the right are the back gardens of houses on Murray Terrace.

The first of many bridges on the line crosses the track at Great Southern Road, and a little further on you find yourself looking down into

INFORMATION

Distance: Culter one way 11km (7 miles), Cults return 10km (6 miles)

Start and finish: Car park in Duthie Park at Polmuir Road entrance.

Terrain: Good track all the way. No special footwear needed.

Public transport: Good bus service from Culter to Aberdeen. Details from Stagecoach Bluebird Buses, Guild Street, Aberdeen (tel: 01224 212266), or from Tourist Information Centre, St Nicholas House, Broad Street, Aberdeen (tel: 01224 288828).

Refreshments: Hotels and cafes at Cults, Culter and elsewhere on North Deeside Road. Exits from rail track at a number of points.

The Subbie Line at Culter Station

Holburn Street. Here, the original bridge that carried trains across was demolished, but there are plans to restore the bridge and also the bridge over the Hardgate for walkers and cyclists. In the meantime, you have to go down to street level by steps to get to the other side and back onto the line.

Holburn Street was an important station in the days of the "subbie" (suburban) trains, disgorging to the West End of the city. It was also the station used by King Edward VII when he broke his holiday at Balmoral in 1906 and travelled from Ballater by train to open extensions to Marischal College at Aberdeen University. Another bridge carries traffic over the line at South Anderson Drive, then it is on past the platforms of Ruthrieston Station until you come to Auchinyell Bridge. Here, the walk begins to move away from the housing areas and out into open country.

A tree-lined section of the walk near Newton Dee

One of the many bridges on the line

The old line goes under a bridge over Pitfodels Station Road (there are steps up to the street) and a little further on are the platforms and the station building, converted for use as a private house. Beyond the station the view opens out. Away on the left the Lower Deeside hills can be seen. Here, the old railway has become a tree-lined avenue and on the right are magnificent houses with beautiful gardens. This was where the city extended when the subbie trains operated – the start of the wealthy "stockbroker belt".

Then the station buildings of Cults loom up. Cults was one of the busiest suburban stations. Back in 1900, one writer commented on how new villas and cottages were turning it into "quite a large village". The clock on the platform has gone, but you can still see where it once ticked away the minutes as passengers – the first of what was to become an army of commuters – waited for the city-bound train. Outside, people park their cars on the station square, and if you want to 'get off' at Cults you can walk up Station Road to the main street for a bus back to the city.

Beyond the station the line crosses a bridge over a steep brae coming down from Cults. Running parallel with it is a turbulent stream, tumbling through the Den of Cults towards the River Dee. From here you can see the river – and sticking up out of it the remains of the Shakkin' Briggie. Its official name was Morison's Bridge, and at one time it was a vital link with folk living on the south side of the Dee, but, lacking proper maintenance, it finally gave way to the wind and weather.

West Cults and Bieldside are next on the line, and on the left are the fairways of Deeside golf course, a popular private course in a lovely setting. Then comes a halt at Murtle, where a road goes up to the Waterwheel Inn. A big stone bridge with railings crosses a road to Murtle House, now occupied by the Rudolf Steiner School.

Birch trees line the track and in season broom and rhododendrons bring a bright splash of colour to the walkway. The next stop is Milltimber, where a road runs down from the A93 to the site of the old station. Milltimber was the nearest station to a well-known hostelry, the Mill Inn at Maryculter, which you can see from the track. Not far from Milltimber a motor road links the North and South Deeside Roads, cutting across the old track. On the other side of the road, the fields and hills to the south open up as you enter the last lap of your walk.

As you approach Culter you go under what seems to be a bridge to nowhere, running into a field. The explanation is that at one time there was a farm on the right (north) side of the railway and the bridge was built so that the farmer could get his cattle over the Deeside line into pasture. The field goes down to the River Dee and for a short distance the track is quite close to it.

Finally, you reach Culter Station – and come to another bridge to nowhere. There are steps up to it and closer inspection shows that, as on the previous bridge, the road over it turned sharp right and went down the other side of the track to St Peter's Church.

The name of the station is still clear on the long, wide platform. Culter was the terminus of the Deeside subbie service. The journey, covering 11 km, took 22 minutes on the "up" trip and 21 minutes on the "down". It is said that its service stood comparison with the London Underground.

Culter Station

To get back to Duthie Park you have to retrace your steps along the line or return to town by a bus from the main street.

Work is proceeding on creating a multi-user Deeside Way route from Aberdeen to Ballater. Walkers will soon be able to extend their outing from Culter to Drumoak, Crathes and Banchory, and still be close to the bus route for the trip back to the city.

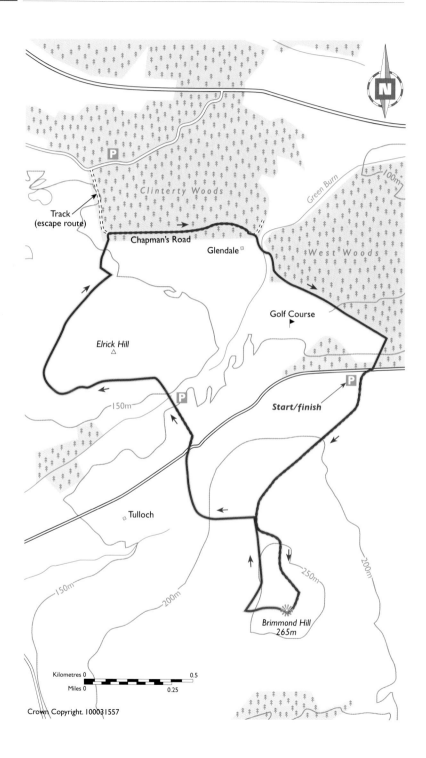

Track
(escape route)

Clinterty Woods

Chapman's Road

Glendale

Green Burn

100m

West Woods

Golf Course

Elrick Hill

Start/finish

150m

Tulloch

150m

200m

250m

200m

Brimmond Hill
265m

Kilometres 0   0.5
Miles 0   0.25

Crown Copyright. 100031557

BRIMMOND AND ELRICK HILL

Brimmond Hill lies on the outer marches of Aberdeen, in the north-west corner of the city. It was from here that watchmen once kept an eye open for a beacon flaring on distant Castlehill, so that their link in the chain could be set alight when invasion was threatened. Now the "invaders" are walkers and bikers, and Brimmond has become a link in another kind of chain – the Four Hills Country Walk.

The Four Hills Walk is a partnership between Aberdeen City Council, the Scottish Agricultural College and the Forestry Commission. At present, it takes in Brimmond Hill (265m/870 ft) and Elrick Hill, but there are plans to extend it to Tyrebagger Hill and the Hill of Marcus. This walk covers part of the Brimmond and Elrick section.

Start at the Brimmond Hill car park on the Bucksburn-Clinterty road. From the car park, go through a gate and walk up a tarred road towards the top of the hill which is crowned by the huge masts of a telecommunications station. Away to the right is the familiar peak of Bennachie, with the sea to the left and the bustle of Aberdeen Airport behind you. On the way up, cross a stile at a gate on the road and after about 300m take the right fork on a wide, roughish track going directly to the top.

From here, you can get a superb bird's eye view of the sea, the city and the surrounding countryside.

INFORMATION

Distance: 6km (3.5 miles) circular.

Start and finish: Brimmond Hill car park. To get there, go by the Lang Stracht or Queen's Road from North Anderson Drive to Kingswells roundabout and turn right to Newhills until you reach a T-junction. Then go left and right again, passing a cemetery. Continue until you reach a crossroads and turn left. The car park is on your left along this road.

Terrain: Good tracks on Brimmond Hill. Steep climb up Elrick Hill. Path down Elrick Hill is narrow and requires care. Strong footwear recommended.

Transport: If you are dropped off by car at Brimmond Hill and want to end the walk at Kirkhill, arrangements should be made to pick you up at the Kirkhill car park off the Tyrebagger. Alternatively, you can take a bus into town from the Tyrebagger road. Times from Stagecoach Bluebird Buses, Guild Street, Aberdeen (Tel. 01224 212266).

View from Brimmond Hill

Near the tall mast is a grassy picnic area with seats and tables and, a short distance away, enclosed by a small dyke, is a curious metal structure which, surprisingly, turns out to be a memorial to the men of Newhills and district who gave their lives in the 1914-18 war. Lift the heavy metal top and underneath is a mountain view indicator.

Between the picnic area and the mast is a waymarker for walkers following the official route, and from here a track goes down the west side of the hill to a fence with a stile over it. From the stile, other paths spin off to the west, one going to a car park near Wynford, but they are not included in this walk. Do not cross the stile but instead turn right alongside the fence by a path which joins a horse trail coming down from the summit. Together, they head towards the tarred road coming up from the car park. Re-cross the stile on the road and continue down the fence line for about 60m to a broad stile into a field. Once over this stile, make your way across and down the field to yet another stile set amongst the trees, which takes you by stone steps on to the Bucksburn – Clinterty road.

Natural sculpture in the woods

Across the road is a track leading to a car park at the foot of Elrick Hill. Elrick is a small hill, but the climb to the top is fairly steep and unsuitable for infirm or elderly people. The first part of the climb is by a flight of steps, then by a rough path to a marker post with yellow arrows pointing round the hill and a brown arrow pointing ahead, directly up the hill. Either follow the brown arrow straight up and over the hill, or preferably turn left onto a narrow footpath (yellow arrow) which skirts the west shoulder of Elrick Hill.

Look out for some unusual features which are part of the Kirkhill Forest Sculpture Trail. When you reach the far side of the hill, the brown arrow route comes in from the right to join up with the yellow route. Go left here and head on an often stony path to a simple seat which looks on to Kirkhill Forest. The forest, which spreads out both north and south of the Tyrebagger road, had its first plantings back in 1922 – Norway spruce, Scots pine, European and Japanese larches, and Douglas fir.

'Sounds of Capercaillie'
sculpture on Elrick Hill

Carry on down past a wooden handrail where there is a drop on the right-hand side to reach a small picnic area with two tables. From here, stone steps take you down through the wood to two modern footbridges over burns with (usually) little water in them. Very shortly, you come out on to a wide forest road. Turn left if you wish to reach the Kirkhill car park and the Tyrebagger road for the bus back to town.

Otherwise, turn right and you are now walking down Chapman's Road. Old records carry frequent references to "the Chapman road" and to a march stone "in an myre at the north syde of the hill of Brimmond".

There is said to be a blocked-up cave in the woods where robbers hid after holding up travellers on the north road. Several more sculptures can be seen on the Chapman's Road, which you should follow until it bends sharp left to a barrier. Here you must turn right and, ignoring a driveway on your right, walk through some fine old conifers to reach a small stone bridge. Cross it and go straight ahead, passing a finger post pointing you uphill to Brimmond. There are lovely old beech trees on your left as you go up beside a burn, passing a wooden bridge.

Follow the line of beech trees, which swing leftwards along the edge of the golf course. Eventually, the path crosses the golf course connecting road into the wood at the other side and heads uphill to come out on the Bucksburn – Clinterty road. Turn right and your car and journey's end are only a few metres along the road.

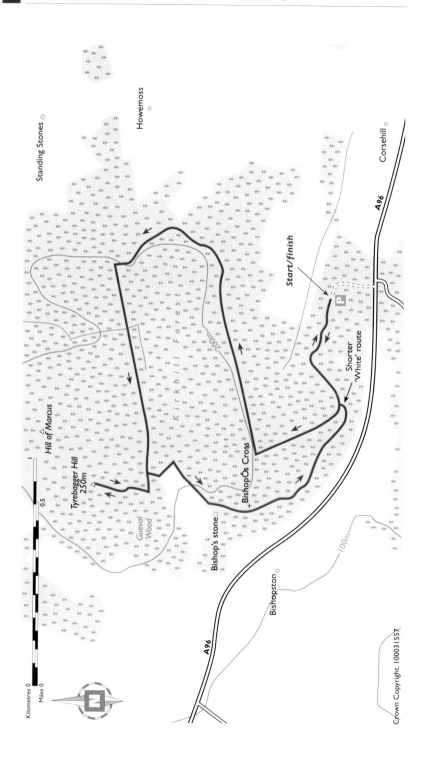

Standing Stones

Howemoss

Hill of Marcus

Tyrebagger Hill
250m

Gueval Wood

Kirkhill Forest

200m

Bishop's stone

+ Bishop's Cross

Start/finish

P

Shorter 'White' route

A96

Corsehill

A96

Bishopston

100m

Kilometres 0
Miles 0
0.5
1

THE TYREBAGGER

This is a walk to the land of Waggles and Woggles. Most people know it as the Tyrebagger, a hill ridge forming a 7km barrier across the route between the sea at Aberdeen and the inland country. When road builders were trying to find a way through the ridge three centuries ago, they were hampered by the boggy terrain – the "woggles" and "waggles". "Woggle" is the old Scots word for a bog, and "waggle" is a quaking bog. There was once a farm called Woggle in Kinellar and a Wagley in Newhills, and Boghead is still a familiar name in the area. The name Tyrebagger is said to come from *tir-bogaire*, "land of the boggy place". Nowadays, a fast dual carriageway takes traffic through the ridge. But Tyrebagger Hill, 821ft (250m) high, offers a pleasant forest walk only a short distance from Aberdeen.

At the end of the parking space, where the track starts, an information board sets out two forest walks – one following white arrows for 5.5km (3.75 miles), the second following yellow arrows for 5km (3 miles). The shorter yellow route covers part of the white route.

Our route is "white", and for the first stretch you may see cyclists in the forest on the right following a mountain bike trail. The main track continues,

INFORMATION

Distance: 7km (4,5 miles) circular.

Start and finish: Tyrebagger car park. To get to the start, follow the A96 Aberdeen to Inverurie road until you are about 1¾ miles (3km) past the roundabout leading to Aberdeen Airport. Turn right here, crossing the carriageway into a dead-end road signed "Forestry Commission – Kirkhill Forest". Then turn left into a large car park.

Terrain: Good tracks. Steepish on last lap to summit. Strong footwear recommended.

Public transport: A regular bus service passes the road from the Tyrebagger car park. Times from Stagecoach Bluebird Buses, Guild Street, Aberdeen (01224 212266).

Refreshments: None en route. Take a flask for a drink on top of the hill.

Looking out from the summit of Tyrebagger Hill

climbing gently, and for a short distance you can spy the countryside over the treetops to the left. Then the forest closes in as you head uphill, the climb becoming steeper. Stick to the main track. Further up you will see a wooden seat where the track goes right and stretches away into the distance in a straight line. Keep following the white arrows, and at a fork keep left, climbing again. Here and there in the woods, you will see posts for orienteers and direction posts for mountain bikers.

Eventually you come to a junction with a post showing a yellow arrow off to the left. This is the shorter walk. Your route however is to the right, following the white arrow up to a T-junction.

The track turns left here and shortly you pass the ruined walls of an old cottage on the right of the track. After about 400m, a white arrow points downhill to the left and this is your return route after you have climbed Tyrebagger Hill. Not far beyond the downhill arrow, a path turns right up the hill – you are on the last lap of the outward walk. The path climbs steeply through the trees, but very soon you will see the stone observation tower on the top.

The stone tower, which has a flight of steps up to a circular viewing platform guarded by railings, was built by a Dr William Henderson of Caskieben. It is about 4m high. The moorland on the west side

Observation tower on Tyrebagger Hill

Please help to keep this place special by:

- Keeping all dogs on a lead or under close control.

- Remaining on footpaths at all times will help to minimise wildlife disturbance.

- Visitors are asked to take all their litter home.

- Strong footwear and waterproofs are recommend-

We hope you have an enjoyable visit. The Rangers will be to answer any questions you might have.

For Ranger guided walks and events please visit: **www.balmoralcastle.com**

Balmoral Ranger service is supporting the Highland Tiger project. Please report any Wild Cat sightings to the website below:

HIGHLAND TIGER
THE SCOTTISH WILDCAT

For information visit highlandtiger.com

Loch Muick Circuit Walk
Prepared by Balmoral Ranger Service

Cairngorms NATIONAL PARK

Balmoral
NEMO · ME · IMPUNE · LACESSIT

Balmoral Estate RANGER SERVICE

Common Butterwort

G

Further on, at
along the track
insectivorous pl
star leaves of t
reddish leaves (
due to tiny red h
The fences alon
are Deer exclos
to help increase
rally regeneratin
area. The heath
favourable cond
tree seeds.
Seedlings are
deer. By prote
have a chance
survive the dam
once the fence
conjunction with
strategy should
tree cover whic
and an increase
wildlife in the Gl

H

As you pass over the wooden bridges of Allt-an-
Dearg, keep your eyes open for Adders. On warm
sunny days they can be seen basking here.

I

When you reach the boathouse you now hav
option of turning right across the top of th
or continuing on the track and turning righ
old stable building.

Both routes will allow you to view the
close range. This area is home to m
ised plants and insects as well as b
nesting and feeding by migratory bi

As you follow the track, the V
come into view marking the end

E

On nearing the South-West end of the
loch, you can see sand and gravel de-
posits scoured from the river bed of the
Allt-an-Dubh Loch which is continually
forming and blocking its own path before
it flows into Loch Muick.

F

The path now leads to the Glas-allt Shiel
house. This house was built for Queen
Victoria when she was in mourning after
Prince Albert's death. If you want to visit
the Glas-allt Falls, take the path directly
from the back of the house up through
the woods– do remember however that
this will add at least an hour to your journey and it is a steep and strenuous path.

Sundew

Waterfall

F

Craig Moseen
706

Glas-allt-Shiel

E

→ Land Rover track
- - - → Footpath (please push

Adder

For more
www.hig

mi
u
S
ed.

We ho
happy

For

of it has been cleared of trees, so that a magnificent panoramic view greets visitors to what is known as the Tappie.

When the Tappie was built in the middle of the 19th century, local folk held an annual Tappie Monday – the first Monday in May, when crowds flocked up the hill to celebrate Tyrebagger's

Expansive view from the Tyrebagger, looking towards Bennachie

answer to the Mither Tap. Sadly, so much damage was done to the tower that Tappie Monday was abandoned, and when the Ordnance Survey revised the map of the district they decided not to put the Tappie back on, in case the May ritual was revived.

Returning down the path from the hilltop, go left down the main track and look for the white arrow mentioned earlier as the return route. Turn right here into what is by far the more attractive half of the Tyrebagger walk. After passing the fields of Gueval Croft you re-enter the woods, and in about 50m, at a post and netting enclosure, a small path goes right, through the trees, to the Bishop's Stone. This is an enormous stone, about 5m long and 3m wide. On it can be seen the initial M and two small cup-shaped holes.

Return to the main track, and downhill there is another link with the Bishop of Aberdeen – a huge cross of stone and turf laid out on the bank to your left and said to mark the boundary of the Bishop's episcopal lands. The track wends its way down through lovely beech trees, although the peace can be a little disturbed by the roar of traffic on the main road below. After a short climb uphill you will rejoin the main track from the car park. Go right here and you will soon be back at the starting point.

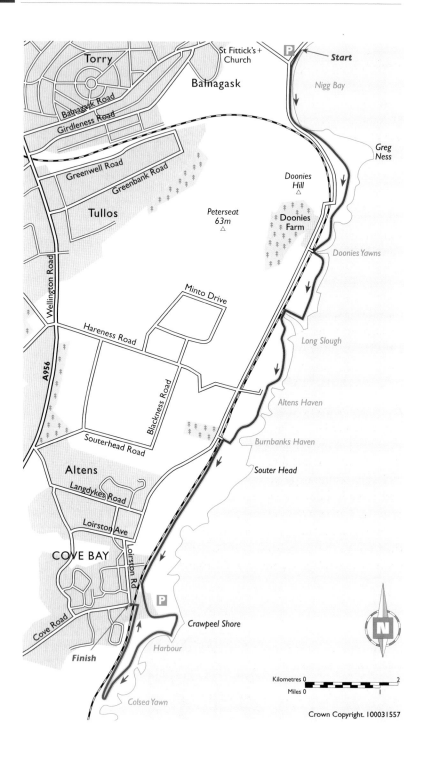

Torry

St Fittick's + Church

Start

Nigg Bay

Balnagask

Balnagask Road

Girdleness Road

Greg Ness

Greenwell Road

Greenbank Road

Doonies Hill △

Tullos

Peterseat 63m △

Doonies Farm

Doonies Yawns

Minto Drive

Long Slough

Hareness Road

Wellington Road

A956

Blackness Road

Altens Haven

Souterhead Road

Burnbanks Haven

Souter Head

Altens

Langdykes Road

Loirston Ave

COVE BAY

Loirston Rd

Crawpeel Shore

Cove Road

Harbour

Finish

Colsea Yawn

Kilometres 0   2
Miles 0   1

N

Crown Copyright. 100031557

NIGG BAY TO COVE

This excellent coastal walk can be started either from Nigg Bay car park or further down the road at Doonies Farm. At Doonies, several rare breeds of animals are kept, including Clydesdale horses, Eriskay ponies and long-horned cattle. This can be a fine attraction for children either before or after their walk.

For the slightly longer route, leave the car at Nigg Bay car park, ensuring it is away from the seaward section of the parking area whenever there is an onshore breeze – it can get very wet from waves breaking over the sea defences.

For a worthwhile start or finish to the walk, visit the ruin of St Fittick's Church, which can be found in the open recreational area on the right from St Fittick's Road when walking towards Nigg Bay. This church and cemetery date from 1199 and are more fully described in Walk 1 of this book (Nigg Bay).

From the car park, look first at the information board erected by the City Council in 1995 when the coast path was developed. Improvements to the path are planned and may have been implemented by the time you take your walk. The footpath initially follows the side of the road past the Scottish Water waste water treatment plant, then a fingerpost indicates where the path diverts from the road. You have already climbed up a little and good views of Nigg Bay are possible, round as far

INFORMATION

Distance: About 4.5 km/3 miles linear, 9km/ 6 miles return.

Start and finish: Bay of Nigg. From Market Street cross Victoria Bridge to Torry; follow Victoria Road to the end of St Fittick's Road, turning right to the Bay of Nigg. An alternative start point is at Doonies Model Farm, which is 1km south of Nigg Bay along the coast road. Car parking is available at both Nigg Bay and Doonies Farm.

Terrain: Typical coastal path, rough in places, with strong footwear recommended. As with all clifftop paths, due care should be taken at all times.

Refreshments: Cafes and shops in Torry and a hotel in Cove.

Toilets: Available at Doonies Farm.

Public Transport: First Direct buses, services 5 and 12, operate between the city centre and Nigg Bay. Service 13 operates to and from Cove.

Opening times: Doonies Farm is open every day except Christmas Day and New Year's Day.

Nigg Bay and Girdleness Lighthouse

as the GirdleNess lighthouse. Some narrow stone barriers have been built to stop cycles and motorcycles from using the path.

Continue along the path noting several concrete sighting posts (Ordnance Survey triangulation points) at intervals along the way. Go past a now redundant coastguard lookout post. There are a number of deep and narrow clefts in the cliff along this stretch of the coast, known variously as yarns or sloughs. These provide suitable nesting ledges, and sea birds can be seen in the springtime in large numbers. The first of these clefts is located down from the traffic lights where the road crosses the railway lines.

There is a damaged section of cliff along here where a considerable landslip has occurred. The footpath avoids the bad ground by heading towards the road for a short distance before returning to the cliff edge.

Clydesdale horses beside the path at Doonies Farm

There is a further information board in the Doonies Farm carpark. To join the coastal path from the farm, cross the rail bridge and follow the signs along a field for about 400m before joining the main coastal path. There is another narrow cleft opposite the farm (Doonies Yawn). Look out for a narrow band of brightly coloured rock visible on the side of the cleft; this band can be seen in several places where clefts occur. The cliffs are an interesting mix of old red sandstone with granite intrusions, sculpted by both sea action and glacial effects. This has helped to produce the long narrow inlets.

The next stretch is rich in wild flowers between April and September. The sandstone cliffs have poor soils with few nutrients, which favours plants such as: northern marsh orchid, heath spotted orchid, meadow vetchling, green alkanet, harebells, bell heather, devil's bit scabious, thrift, lesser stitchwort and red campion. In the sea, dolphins can often be seen, so keep looking around you for different types of flora and fauna. As you approach the Altens Industrial Estate there are signs of derelict wartime installations, now all but disappeared. Sea caves can also be seen in the Long Slough cleft in the cliffs.

Continue past derelict cottages, and an A-frame and wire structure which was used until about 1999 in association with the salmon fishing. The catches were winched to the top of the cliffs from the boats below. This is also close to the old fishing village of Burnbank, where there is another access point to the road and some limited car parking.

Approaching Cove village, look out for more caves and nesting sea birds. Eventually you find the final fingerpost pointing up away from the coast. Follow this along the side of a dyke to a track where you turn left (do not cross the railway line here) and which then leads directly into the village. Go past the hotel, where refreshments can be obtained, and continue on Colsea Road, through the old part of the village. For an easy return to Aberdeen, a no. 13 bus can be caught from just over the railway bridge in the centre of the village. However, it is worth continuing down Colsea Road to the old harbour, still used by some shellfish boats.

Doonies Yawn

From the harbour, either go back along Colsea Road to the village, or, for the fitter walkers, there is a strenuous climb up from the harbour skirting the cliffs and onto a narrow path along the top of the cliffs. After about 500m this takes you to Colsea Yawn, a very deep and narrow cleft, but well worth visiting. It is not possible to go beyond here, but go up to the railway line to join a track back to the village.

You can then either take the bus back to Aberdeen, or return by the coastal path.

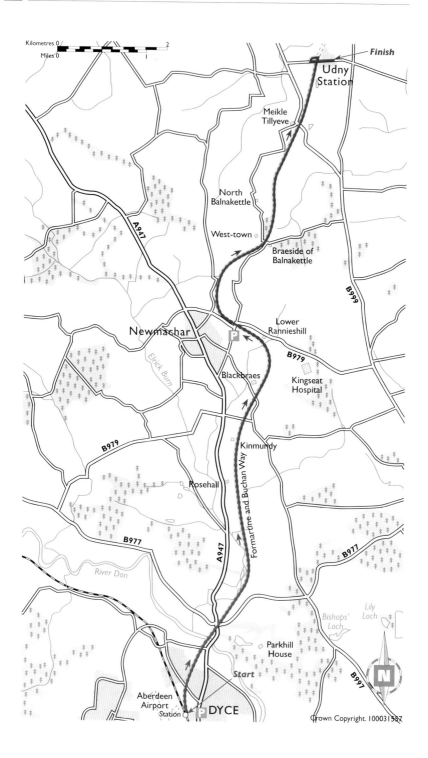

Kilometres 0 2
Miles 0 1

Finish

Udny Station

Meikle Tillyeve

North Balnakettle

West-town

Braeside of Balnakettle

A947

B999

Newmachar

Lower Rannieshill

P

B979

Blackbraes

Kingseat Hospital

Elrick Burn

B979

Kinmundy

Rosehall

Formartine and Buchan Way

A947

B977

River Don

B977

Lily Loch

Bishops' Loch

Parkhill House

Start

B997

Aberdeen Airport Station

P DYCE

N

Crown Copyright. 100031557

THE FORMARTINE AND BUCHAN WAY: DYCE TO UDNY

For about 100 years, trains ran through rural Aberdeenshire towards Fraserburgh and Peterhead. These routes were closed in the 1960s and trains now only run north from Aberdeen to Inverness. But the loss of the trains has offered great opportunities to open up the old routes for walkers, cyclists and horse riders. This walk uses the southern section of the Formartine and Buchan Way, from Dyce as far as Udny Station, from where a bus can be caught for the return trip back to Aberdeen; alternatively a walk back along the outward route makes a fine outing. Why not complete the rail experience by taking the train from Aberdeen out to Dyce to start the walk?

The route starts from Dyce station car park. The path is well marked, especially since the section as far as Newmachar coincides with National Cycle Network (Sustrans) route 1. Serious cyclists could take route 1 all the way to John o' Groats and on to Orkney and Shetland, while walkers need to be content with more limited horizons.

Setting off along the path, you initially pass through an industrial estate, and you soon become aware of the proximity of Aberdeen Airport. Helicopters regularly pass overhead as they make their way to, or return from, the offshore North Sea Platforms. This activity is soon left behind and

INFORMATION

Distance: Dyce to Udny Station, one way 13 km (8 miles)

Start and finish: Car park at Dyce railway station; from the city, follow signs to Dyce, take Victoria Road and turn left down Station Road to the station. Alternatively, travel from Aberdeen to Dyce by train. From Udny Station either take the 290 or 291 bus back to Aberdeen or walk back the way you came.

Terrain: Newly constructed path along the old railway line, good surface and mainly level walking with only gentle inclines.

Toilets: In Dyce.

Refreshments: Hotels in Dyce plus hotel at Udny Station.

Public Transport: Good city bus service out to Dyce and Stagecoach Bluebird service 290/291 return from Udny Station. Regular trains from Aberdeen to Dyce.

The River Don bridge

you reach the footbridge over Riverview Drive, where there is alternative access and some limited parking. It is a pleasure to walk, unhindered, high above the busy road without having to pause to avoid the traffic.

A little further on you cross the River Don on a fine granite bridge; here you may see salmon and sea trout on their migrations from the sea. The third bridge is again over a major road crossing at Parkhill. Look for the colourful milepost erected as a millennium project to mark the creation of the National Cycle Network. There is disabled access to the Way here at Parkhill.

Old railway lines offer valuable corridors for wildlife, linking isolated woods and mosses, crossing waterways and marshy areas which provide sanctuary for many plants and animals. Deer, fox, weasel and stoat all use the line and numerous badger setts are found close to and, occasionally, on it. Early morning is the best time to see them, or at dusk, when bats also flit between the trees in summer. Daytime sightings are always a possibility, though, and keen ears may pick up shrews darting through the grasses and froglets in damper areas of vegetation.

National Cycle Network milepost

Much of the line is flanked with rosebay willowherb – also known as "fireweed" – spread far and wide by the railway. Bees love it and the line's many flowering plants are a great place to spot different types of bumblebee, hoverflies and beetles. Many flowers lost due to intensive farming are widespread on the line – such as harebells and oxeye daisies, yellow toadflax, foxglove and St John's wort, red campion, cat's ear and heady scented meadowsweet. Some rarities such as crosswort, tutsan, orpine and long-stalked cranesbill might also be seen.

As you continue northwards look to your left, westwards, to see Bennachie and, far beyond, the higher hills of the eastern Cairngorms coming into view. But this area is mainly agricultural, and various crops and animals will be seen in the adjacent fields. The ground is gently rising as you approach Newmachar, about 1km to the west. There is a long bend around to the left and on the right here you see the buildings of Kingseat Hospital.

Just north of Newmachar is another access point with parking. This is where the National Cycle Route leaves the Way and continues in a more westerly direction. Notice the old platforms which formed Newmachar station, now all but absorbed into the adjacent house gardens.

Some distance further on you reach a deep cutting. Here, back in the 1960s, a train was "lost" for some time when it ploughed into a large snowdrift. Beyond the cutting, the top of the rise is reached and the view to the north suddenly opens out, giving excellent views of the Aberdeenshire countryside. In winter the adjacent fields often attract noisy redwing and fieldfare which have migrated from Scandinavia.

Easy walking on the old line near Newmachar

As you walk along the line, look out for Tillycorthie Mansion through the trees to the right. This beautiful private home was built in 1911 and was one of the first Scottish mansions to be built of concrete.

Keep a look out for ducks, swans and hunting dragonflies on a man-made pond just south of Udny Station. Pass beneath a bridge and turn right again, back over the bridge and into the village. There is a pub here for refreshment but, sadly, the Muffin and Crumpet Bistro has been closed for several years.

You can catch the no. 290 or 291 service bus here back to Aberdeen or simply reverse your route and walk back along the line to Dyce, enjoying the views in the opposite direction as you leave the countryside and approach the airport and the city.

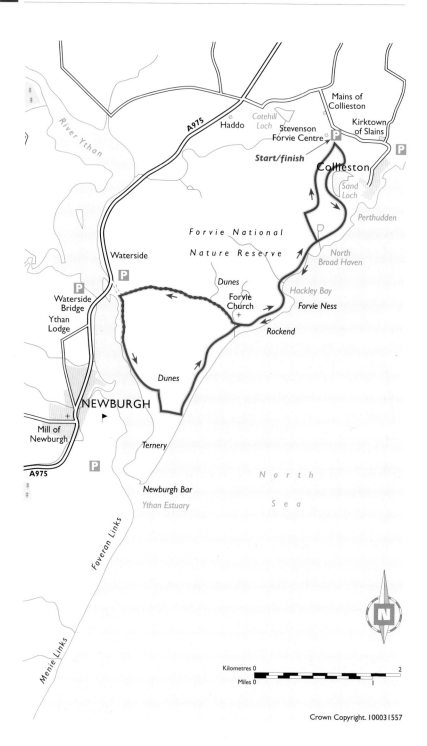

Mains of
Collieston

Kirktown
of Slains

Cotehill Loch

Haddo

Stevenson
Forvie Centre

A975

River Ythan

Start/finish

Collieston

Sand Loch

Perthudden

F o r v i e   N a t i o n a l

N a t u r e   R e s e r v e

Waterside

Dunes

Forvie
Church

North Broad Haven

Hackley Bay

Forvie Ness

Waterside
Bridge

Ythan
Lodge

Rockend

Dunes

NEWBURGH

Mill of
Newburgh

Ternery

A975

Newburgh Bar

Ythan Estuary

N o r t h

S e a

Foveran Links

Menie Links

N

Kilometres 0   2

Miles 0   1

Crown Copyright. 100031557

THE SANDS OF FORVIE

Yf evyr madenis malysone
Dyd licht upon drye land
Let nocht bee funde in Furvy's glebys
Bot thystl, bent and sande.

That ancient curse comes to mind when you walk the "thystl, bent and sande" on the coastline between Collieston and Newburgh. It is said to have been brought down on the head of a Laird of Forvie who cast his three daughters adrift so that they would be denied their inheritance. But the curse turned out to be a blessing, for today Forvie has become one of Scotland's most important National Nature Reserves.

To explore "Furvy's glebys", it is best to start at the Stevenson Forvie Centre, a short distance off the road to Collieston. The Centre has excellent displays inside and will show you on request a short film about the Reserve. The Reserve, which was opened in January 1959, is now largely owned and managed by Scottish Natural Heritage and takes in the fifth largest sand dune system in Britain.

At the Centre, a sign points the way along a path leading into the Reserve. Away on the left, you can see a row of old fishermen's cottages just outside Collieston. After going through a kissing gate, bear left, heading towards the cottages.

Forvie Reserve

Black-headed gulls squawk overhead as you come to the Sand Loch. A gravel path takes you round the head of the loch, where white bog-cotton serves as a reminder that the land here is marshy. The path comes out near a football field, where there is a gate near the main coastal track from Collieston, the route you will follow. Here, there is a board with information – and a map – on Forvie, including the estuary, which is an optional extra on this walk.

Now you are heading south along the cliff-tops. Herring gulls jostle for breeding sites on the cliffs, kittiwakes can be seen perched on precarious corners of the rocks, and fulmars, which make guttural growling noises and spit foul-smelling oil at you, glide effortlessly along the cliff-tops.

Offshore, great rafts of eiders bob about on the water. They are the best-known birds at Forvie; not surprisingly, since some 5,000 of them come

Part of the extensive dune system at Forvie

A six-spot burnet moth
on a harebell

to the area each summer. Those with the spectacular plumage are the males!

You soon reach a brown marker post. The path to
the right is your return route, so keep going straight
ahead. The path dips down over wet marshland,
duckboarding carrying you over it and duckboard
steps climbing up from it. The steps are steep and
need a little care.

The path narrows as you approach beautiful
Hackley Bay, whose golden sands attract many pic-
nickers. Here, duckboards go gently roller-coasting
round the top of the bay, taking you over the awk-
ward stretches. When you reach the south side, there
are steps down if you wish to reach the sand and a
warning notice about high tide times.

Beyond Hackley Bay, you begin to see the great
sweep of sand round to the Ythan estuary and
beyond that to Balmedie and Aberdeen. Now
you come to another brown marker post. Turn
right along a narrow path that will take you to
the remains of Forvie Kirk, built in the 12th
century on the site of a chapel believed to date
back to AD 704.

This is all that remains of a settlement that was
buried by the sand in the Middle Ages. In 1951,
the foundations of a village of 19 circular huts,
2,000 years old, were discovered under the sand.

It was, say superstitious folk, all the result of the "madenis malysone", the curse uttered by the three daughters of the Laird of Forvie. At any rate, the "lost" village put the Sands of Forvie on the map.

Beyond the ruined kirk, a path takes you over a burn to a track running down to the Ythan estuary and to Newburgh. If, however, you prefer to turn back at this point, go left to the former salmon fishing station at Rockend, a short distance along the main track.

Rockend is a nice spot to have your picnic, looking up along the bay to the mouth of the Ythan. It is also the point from which you start your return journey. First, however, let's look at the alternative.

Turn right on the main track away from the sea, cross over the dune heathland and walk down to reach the Ythan estuary, where you should turn left and head towards the sea again. Across the water is Newburgh, where the Culterty Field Centre, run by Aberdeen University zoology department, puts the birdlife of Buchan under the scientist's microscope.

Four species of tern breed among the sand dunes at the south end of the estuary. The most numerous is the Sandwich tern; there is a breeding colony of up to 1,500 pairs in the ternery. There is also a colony of up to 50 pairs of little tern, one of Britain's rarest breeding seabirds. The elegant flight and spectacular diving of the terns can be seen as you walk up the estuary, where they feed on sand eels and other small fish. The ternery is cordoned off during the breeding season between April and August.

Walk to the end of the boardwalk following the blue arrows and cut through the dunes to the beach. The route is easily followed, and once on the beach you continue down the sands to Rockend.

Ducks and ducklings parade on the sand

From Rockend, make your way back to the Forvie Centre, passing the path that went off to Forvie Kirk. Watch out for the second brown marker post after Hackley Bay. Turn left here on the alternative route back to the Centre which takes you past a small lochan, a favourite haunt of ducks and gulls. On your way back, keep an eye open for roe deer. There are more than a dozen on the Reserve. Other markers will lead you through the heathland on the twisty path to the Centre.

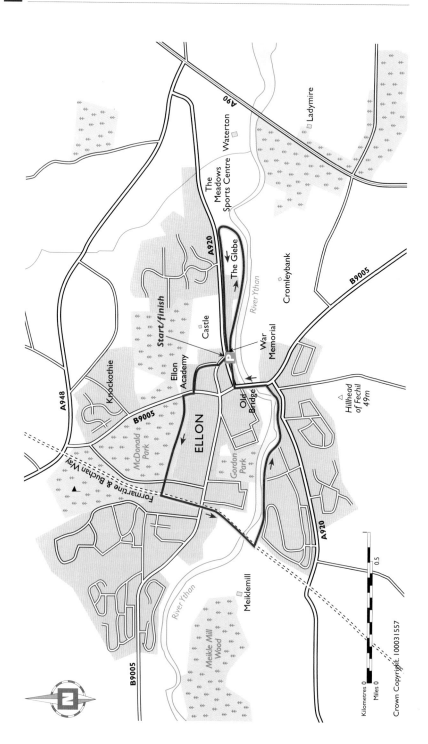

Crown Copyright. 100031557

ELLON

Two bridges span the River Ythan at Ellon – one old, one new. In a way they are symbolic, for the 'capital' of Buchan is a modern town that still has one foot in the past. The oil boom turned it into a commuter-satellite of Aberdeen, but it retains its own distinctive character.

This walk starts in the shadow of Ellon's twin bridges – in the car park at Market Street, on the edge of the river. This was where the Moot Hill, now gone, once dominated the town, and where the Earls of Buchan held court and dispensed justice. The path in front of the car park, decorated with tall, elegant lamp-posts, strikes out in both directions, clinging to the riverbank, but you go left, with back gardens and houses on one side and the river and open countryside on the other.

Not very far along the path you go through a gate and enter the Glebe. This is a pleasant area of parkland, trim with trees and bushes, where you can sit and watch the river – and the world – go by. Just past the gate a short track goes up to Castle Road, the A920 to Peterhead and Fraserburgh. This is where you leave the park a little later.

The path through the Glebe takes you to a point where a narrower path goes off to the right and the main path goes left to another Castle Road exit. Stick to the narrow, right-hand path, which crosses a wooden bridge over a dried-up burn and heads towards Ellon cemetery. Keep going right by paths that take you to the riverside.

The Meadows Sports Centre can be seen ahead, with steps leading up to it, but before you come to it, turn left into a neatly laid out car park. The road into the car park comes down from Castle Road, while another

INFORMATION

Distance: 5 km (3 miles) circular.

Start and finish: Market Street car park, Ellon (over the bridge and turn right at roundabout). Ellon is 24km (15 miles) north of Aberdeen on the A90.

Toilets: In Market Street car park.

Terrain: Roads, paths and old Buchan railway line. No special footwear usually needed, but the riverside path can be muddy after rain.

Refreshments: Ice cream shop across from car park. Good pubs and restaurants nearby.

Public transport: Stagecoach Bluebird Service 260-263 from Aberdeen. For information, tel: 01224 212266.

Old and new bridges

dead-end road – Meadows Way – leads to a housing estate on the Meadows. When you walk the banks of the Ythan you can see fishermen casting their lines, but once they "fished" for something more profitable – pearls. The Ythan was famous for its pearls.

There are two choices awaiting you at the Glebe car park. You can go up to Castle Road and walk into town on the next leg of the walk, or – a bonnier alternative – you can retrace your steps through the Glebe, sticking to the higher path. There are three exit/entrances to the Glebe on Castle Road, but it is best to go back to the gate where you entered and leave the park there.

Head for the war memorial, which is about 200 yards down Castle Road. Bear right by an old drinking trough where there is an inscription, "For the refreshment of weary beasts". Turn sharp right up Schoolhill Road, passing Ellon Academy, which stands in a setting of trees and grassland. Turn right again up Golf Road and cross at the pedestrian lights. Beside the crossing is the entrance to McDonald Park.

Obelisk in McDonald Park

The long, tree-lined avenue through the park runs alongside Ellon golf course, but a little way up a stone obelisk in the middle of the track bars the way. Its inscription reads, "This park was presented to the burgh of Ellon in 1928 by James Gordon McDonald of Rhodesia who lived within sight of this monument for over sixty years."

It is a lovely walk, passing a small rockery (with seats) presented to the town, but it looks as if they made a habit of putting up obstacles on the avenue, for farther on a huge stone blocks the way. McDonald of Rhodesia has been at it again. He had the stone put there to mark the Coronation of George VI and Queen Elizabeth (later the Queen Mother) in May 1937.

The avenue ends and you leave the park and turn right past a council depot. At the far end of the depot, cross the road and take the path alongside the depot, heading west. At the end of the path go up some paved steps or the adjacent ramp leading to a dusty track on the edge of a housing estate. You are now on the Formartine and Buchan Way, a footpath and cycleway using the old railway line to Maud and beyond.

Follow the Way until it goes down to the right and decants you onto a street near Station Road. Turn left and then left again on Station Road, and the continuation of the Way can be seen on the opposite side of the street, marked by a wooden fence and a gate.

Climb up onto the Way and you get a train driver's view of the Buchan countryside. Marathon walkers who decide to carry on will end up in Dyce. Not far ahead is a railway bridge over the Ythan. From it you can see a wooden pedestrian bridge downstream, linking the north and south banks of the river.

There are steps down to the riverbank at both ends of the bridge. Skip the first steps. Those at the far end of the bridge are rough and fairly steep, so be careful. They take you onto a tarmac path running alongside the river, which is fringed with a variety of trees including gean, sycamore, fir and alder.

You can cross the pedestrian bridge and go back to the car park on the north bank, but much more satisfying is the route by the south bank. The path winds along the river bank and at the back of a new housing development. Before reaching the twin bridges, you can leave the path by steps going up to the hotel. Otherwise, it's under the "new" bridge, with the roar of traffic above you, and a climb up a steep slope to the old bridge. The Auld Brig, as it is affectionately known, was built in 1793 and is a Category A listed building.

The River Ythan

It looks good for another couple of centuries. No traffic here; only human feet cross its ancient surface. Out past the bollards at the north end and you are in busy Ellon again, only a few steps away from your car.

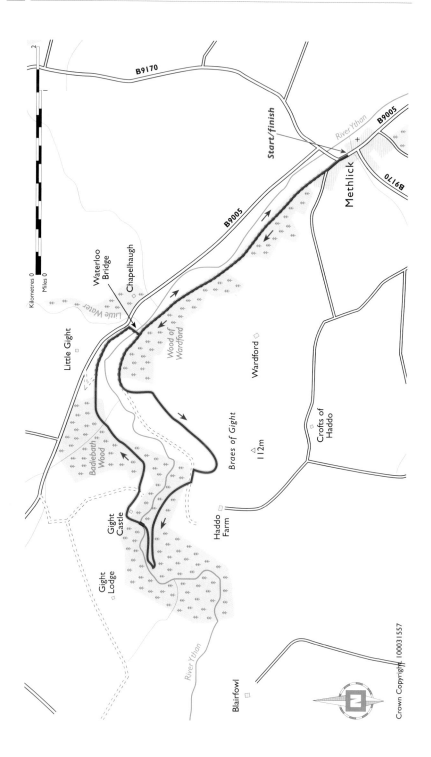

Kilometres 0
Miles 0

B9170

Start/finish

River Ythan

B9005

Methlick

B9170

B9005

Waterloo
Bridge

Chapelhaugh

Little Water

Little Gight

Wood of
Wardford

Wardford

Braes of Gight

Crofts of
Haddo

112m

Badiebath
Wood

Gight Castle

Haddo
Farm

Gight
Lodge

River Ythan

Blairfowl

Crown Copyright 100031557

THE BRAES O' GIGHT

The Braes of Gight (locally pronounced 'Gicht') provide the setting for this outing – a walk through lovely countryside where the poet Byron's ancestors had their home. Here, you can walk in the footsteps of the "wild Gordons"and look at the gaunt ruins of the castle where they lived.

The walk starts in the village of Methlick. When you set off, turn right from the car park and go along the main street until it swings right towards the River Ythan. Your way lies straight ahead, so cross the street to where a cobbled area at the junction is decorated with an old millstone. Keeping left of the millstone, take the road past the public hall (built 1908), leaving it a little further on to follow a track going through a builder's yard into the woods. There is a wire barrier across it to keep cars out.

Beech trees line one side of the track, but on your left the hill is bare. The sound of gunfire can sometimes be heard, but no one is hunting the roe deer that can often be seen in the forest. The shots are from the Kingscliff Shooting Lodge, across the river, where clay pigeon shooting ranges are laid out.

INFORMATION

Distance: 9.5km (6 miles) circular.

Start and finish: Main Street car park in Methlick. Take the A90 from Aberdeen to Ellon and the B9005 from Ellon to Methlick. The village is about 13km (8 miles) northwest of Ellon.

Toilets: In car park.

Terrain: Good track for much of the way, but the section at the western end of the walk is boggy but open where tree felling has been carried out. Steep climb up to Gight Castle from the Ythan. The Castle can be approached by a shorter and more direct route from a parking area near the Waterloo Bridge. Strong footwear recommended.

Refreshments: Shops and pubs in the village.

Public transport: Stagecoach Bluebird service 290 or 291 to Methlick. For information, tel: 01224 212266.

Old millstone in Methlick

When you come to a fork in the track, the right-hand leg goes down to the Waterloo Bridge, an impressive name for a wee brig in a back-of-beyond spot in Buchan. Near the bridge a stream called the Little Water runs into the Ythan. It is also known as the Black Water of Gight, and there is a spot on the river called the Black Stank. Stank is a Scots word for a pool. The Ythan throws up a number of curious place-names as you follow its course: downstream from the Waterloo Bridge is the Gowkie's Pot, while upstream is Meg's Pot. A gowk is a cuckoo and a pot is a pool.

Your route is not over Waterloo Bridge (you re-turn by it later), but straight ahead by the left fork. There are a number of gates on the walk and after going through the second one the track moves away from the river and climbs gently uphill.

Soon you come to a second fork. Ignore the left leg, which leads to Haddo Farm. Instead, go straight ahead through another gate, which opens into a field where cattle may be grazing, and follow the track as it runs along the edge of the wood. The track has a new barbed wire fence alongside. Even-tually you reach a fifth gate where the wire fence turns and no longer follows the track. Go through this gate (please remember to shut all gates behind you).

Rope bridge for red squirrels across the Ythan

Beyond the fifth gate the track continues through dense Forestry Commission woodland. This track has been improved to allow heavy vehicles to ex-tract timber. About 50m beyond the gate, just be-fore a turning circle, a grassy path goes down through trees to the right. Ignore this path and continue on the track. When you come to a wide open space at the end of the tree-line, you have reached the turning point of the walk. There is a huge rock face on your left.

Turn right here and follow a path down to the

river. The route now does a U-turn and follows the Ythan downstream, running parallel with the outward track. Following the tree clearance it is easy to find a route, preferably close to the river bank, though it is rough and boggy in places. As you reach the river, look up to see a rope bridge. It allows red squirrels to cross the river from the pines over to the hazel trees where they can find one of their favourite foods. You pass a wooden bridge over the river, but ignore this and continue along the bank until you reach the next wooden bridge, which is situated below Gight Castle. This bridge was lifted in by helicopter in 1996.

High above the river in this picturesque spot you will get your first glimpse of Gight Castle, its gaunt ruins perched almost on the edge of a deep drop to the river. After crossing the bridge a narrow path takes you to the top. It is a steep climb, but well

Gight Castle

worth the effort, for wild flowers bloom on the brae and on your way up you will have a magnificent view of the countryside, with the Ythan winding its way through the valley below. The woodlands stretching into the distance seem to mock the old taunt about "treeless Buchan".

On top of the path, where a stile takes you over a fence to the castle, there is a Scottish Wildlife Trust notice welcoming you to Gight Woods. The Trust bought part of the Gight lands and have planted native species such as wild cherry (gean), oak and ash. From the path you can see the Prop of Ythsie, a lofty tower which dominates the countryside between Pitmedden and Haddo House. It was built in memory of George Gordon, 4th Earl of Aberdeen, who was Prime Minister from 1852 to 1855.

The Gordons who lived in Gight Castle also won a place in the history books, but for different reasons. Sitting above the Ythan, under the ruins of this grim Catholic stronghold, you will probably ask yourselves the same question that was put in a verse by the famous seer, Thomas the Rhymer:

> *Twa men sat down on Ythan brae,*
> *The ane did to the ither say,*
> *"An' what sic men may the Gordons o' Gight*
>   *hae been?"*

The answer is violent, lawless men. They were known as the wild Gordons of Gight and their dynasty was "crowded with murder and sudden death". Thomas the Rhymer also wrote a prophetic couplet:

> *When the herons leave the tree,*
> *The lairds o' Gight shall landless be.*

That prophecy came true in the time of Catherine Gordon, mother of the poet Byron. Catherine was the unlucky 13th in this tragic line. Her husband – the poet's father – was Mad Jack Byron, who gambled away the family fortunes. When she used the last of her money to pay her husband's debts, the herons deserted Gight and crossed the Ythan to settle on Lord Aberdeen's land.

Down below the castle there is another "pot" in the Ythan with an unsavoury reputation – Hagberry Pot. One of the Lairds of Gight hid his treasure in this pool, and when he ordered a servant to go down for it, the man refused because he thought the Devil was at the bottom. In fact, the name of the pool is innocent enough, for hagberry is a tree also called the bird cherry, which can be seen growing on the Gight braes.

Gight Castle was built about 1560 by the second Gordon laird. It must have been a mighty stronghold, but it is a sad sight now. Outside it a notice warns that the structure is dangerous. There is an

Another view of Gight Castle

intriguing little stone beside a wall of the castle. The inscription on it reads "Lady Sneddon, Oct 81 to April 94", but there is nothing to show whose pet dog is buried in the shadow of the old castle.

Look for another stone – an old milestone – near the castle. The faded inscription reads 'HH 5' – Haddo House 5 miles. From here, follow a track leading to a gate which will put you on the road back to Methlick. It runs through lovely woodland until you come to a bridge over the Burn of Stonehouse. A short distance beyond the bridge, the track runs up to the main Fyvie road, cutting through another denuded hill, but your way is to the right, following the Ythan. Across the river you will see the track you started out on, with the first of the devastated treeless hills behind it.

Soon you will see the Waterloo Bridge ahead. The track runs on to join the Fyvie road near the bridge, but before you come to it you will pass a small car park on the left. This is used by fishermen, but weekend walkers also park there on their way to Gight Castle. For those who want a direct route to Gight, without going up the west side of the Ythan, this is a good place to start.

When you reach the Methlick-Fyvie road, turn right over the Waterloo Bridge, then left, and soon you are back in the village.

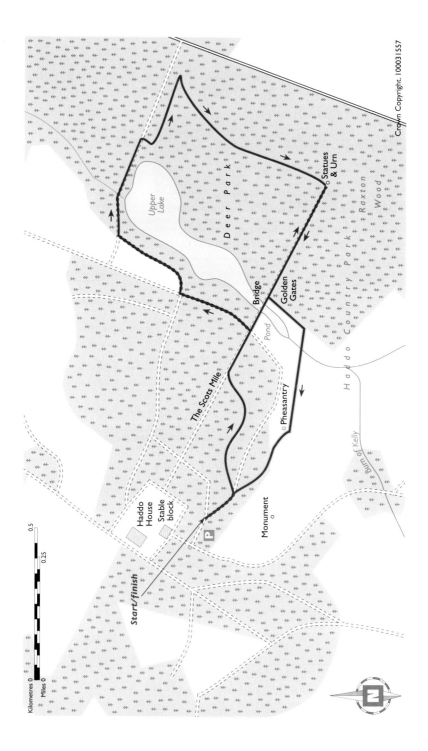

Crown Copyright. 10003 l557

Upper Lake

Deer Park

Statues & Urn

Raxton Wood

Haddo Country Park

Bridge

Golden Gates

Pond

The Scots Mile

Pheasantry

Haddo House

Stable block

Monument

Burn of Kelly

P

Start/finish

Kilometres 0

Miles 0

0.25

0.5

N

HADDO HOUSE AND PARK

When you wander through Haddo Country Park, you are walking in the footsteps of a host of famous people – Queen Victoria, Gladstone and Lord Rosebery; Sir George Otto Trevelyan, the historian and biographer; George du Maurier, the novelist, and many more.

The country park came into being in 1978, when Haddo House and its garden were transferred to the care of the National Trust for Scotland. At the same time, 180 acres of land were given to Aberdeenshire Council to establish a park. Today, it is a magnet for thousands of visitors.

Before you set off, look for an information board at one end of the parking area. It carries a big map of the country park. To the right of it, a few stone steps lead up to a path which curves round to the right. This is the start of your walk.

On your right as you set off is a tall obelisk built by George Gordon, 4th Earl of Aberdeen, in memory of his brother Arthur, who was killed at the Battle of Waterloo in 1815. The monument is not in fact in the country park, but a path from the car park leads to it.

The trees bend their branches in salute as you go through the woods. If you tried to name them all

INFORMATION

Distance: 5km (3miles) circular.

Start and finish: Haddo House car park. To get to Haddo House, take the A90 north from Aberdeen, branching off at Murcar on the B999 to Pitmedden and Tarves. Before reaching Tarves, look for National Trust for Scotland signs directing you to Haddo House.

Terrain: Good surfaces all the way. Strong footwear recommended.

Toilets: Stable block at Haddo House and Pheasantry building.

Refreshments: Tearoom in Stable block, also souvenir shop.

Public Transport: Stagecoach Bluebird buses run to the road end. Service 290, 291 (tel 01224 212266).

Opening hours: Haddo House and Stable block: open Easter to end of October. Phone 01651 851440 for exact times. Closed in winter. Pheasantry toilets open all year round. Haddo Country Park: open all year, daily 0930–sunset.

Haddo House

you would have your work cut out, for there are 70 species of trees and shrubs here, from a horse chestnut – the familiar "conkers" tree – near the Stable block to mighty beeches and aspen which have grown at Haddo for hundreds of years. There are wooden signs identifying the trees.

The short path from the car park joins one of the main surfaced roads from the Stable block. Follow the blue arrow, and when you come to a fork, leave the surfaced road and go left, through an area where jackdaws nest in the spring. Through the trees on the right is a red-brick building. Have a guess at what it is – you'll find the answer on the way back!

Soon you are at a crossroads. Here, on your left, a long avenue runs down from Haddo House, while on the right it stretches away to the Deer Park. This avenue is known as the Scots Mile. There are actually two avenues, one being the Victoria Avenue planted to mark Queen Victoria's Jubilee, and together they measure a Scots mile – 1984 imperial yards (about 2km). A "normal" mile is 1760 yards.

Go right at the crossroads. Shortly, a blue arrow points you into the woods on the left along a lovely path through a small woodland on the edge of the lake, passing a number of pools where frogs and toads spawn. Their numbers are apparently declining – at one time there were notices warning people that there were frogs crossing.

The path takes you on to a wide track which, as you turn right, runs up the side of the Upper Lake, opening out to give you a good view over the water. Watch for a sign on the right indicating a path to a bird hide. At a T-junction, go right and round the head of the lake, where a wooden platform with a fence juts out into the water. Here, swans will come to the platform to be fed. There is a lifebelt in case you fall in!

The track curves round the top of the lake and, turning back, crosses a wooden bridge over the Burn of Kelly. Beyond the bridge, turn left and head onto a smooth grassy path towards the high dyke enclosing the deer park, which dates back to 1690. The dyke once penned in a herd of fallow deer, and there are two statues of fallow deer at the top of the Deer Park. The fallow deer have long since gone (they were replaced by Highland cattle in 1898), but if you are lucky you may see wild roe deer coming out of the woods.

The path bends right and goes uphill, and at the top of the dyke, near an old gateway, turns right again and undulates along pleasantly with a conifer wood on the left. When you reach an open area, you will see the deer statues on your left with, beyond, a huge urn perched on an equally massive pedestal. It was erected by the 4th Earl of Aberdeen, in memory of his first wife. The 4th Earl was Prime Minister from 1852 to 1855. He was a moderate Prime Minister but a good laird, for at Haddo he brought a neglected estate back to life, planting 14 million trees before he died.

Top: Fallow deer statue
Above: Memorial urn to Lady Aberdeen

From the top of the Deer Park, you get an impressive view down the Scots Mile to Victoria Avenue and Haddo House. Make your way down the broad grassy avenue of the Scots Mile to reach the Golden Gates, the name given to the magnificent black and gold gates carrying the Gordon coat of arms. Once through the gates, turn immediately left and, after crossing a burn by a small wooden bridge, you will see a post pointing you left to a path cut through an area of rough grass. Where the rough grass gives way to a mown field, another post points in the direction of a gap in the trees on the far side of the field.

As you cross the field, you will see away to the right the red-brick building you passed at the start of the walk. A path runs down to steps leading to the front of the building. Have you guessed what it is?

On one of the doors there is a sign, "The Old Pheasantry", and it is known as the Pheasantry Building. There seems to be some doubt about whether or not it ever housed pheasants, although today the estate rears about 10,000 pheasants each year for shooting.

Incidentally, the wooden pheasant signs you see have nothing to do with the Pheasantry or with rearing pheasants. They mark the boundary between the Country Park and the estate, which carries on the business of farming, forestry and game.

But back to the Pheasantry. This stylish building was constructed in 1885 – as a hen house! That, at any rate, is what some people say and local folk actually speak about it as the Poultry Yard. According to a Ranger Service leaflet, the locals claim that "it never saw anything more glamorous than a Rhode Island Red". The Rangers would love to know the true story.

The Old Pheasantry

Today, the building is used by local scouts and by the Park's Ranger Service, who work with schools, disabled groups, senior citizens and other clubs. There are toilets inside. Leaving the Pheasantry, follow the blue-arrow path back to the stable block and the car park. Note the tennis court on the right – you can book a game there. There is also an adventure playground in the park.

Before you leave the Country Park, it is worthwhile taking a look at Haddo House (see Information for details) and the garden laid out there when the famous house, designed by William Adam, was built in 1732. It fell into disrepair, but in 1805 the 4th Earl renovated it with the artist and landscape gardener James Giles.

There is a final reminder of the 4th Earl's contribution to Haddo when you leave the estate. On the hill of Ythsie, between Haddo and Pitmedden, there is a tall stone monument known as the Prop of Ythsie. The word "prop" means a landmark, and this one was built as a memorial to the 4th Earl. It is well worth a visit. It is said, not without justification, that from here you get the best view in Buchan.

There are other walks to be followed and other things to see. Haddo Country Park is, without doubt, a magical place.

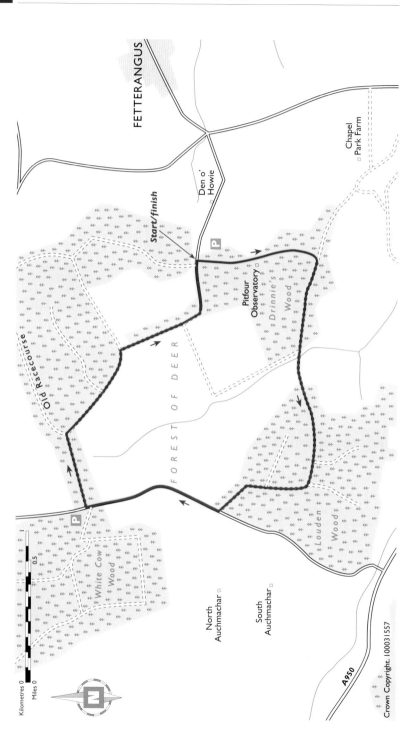

PITFOUR

I t's off to the races on this walk – to see where a north-east laird once held his own Ascot in the heart of Buchan. From a tall tower in Drinnie's Wood, near Fetterangus, the laird and his guests may have watched their horses galloping around a circular racecourse laid out on the high ground above Cairnorchies.

At Fetterangus, signposts point the way to a car park and a small but attractive picnic area a short distance west of the village. From the picnic area a track leads through a stretch of moorland to the Pitfour Observatory, which is open from Easter to mid-October.

The Observatory, an octagonal, three-storey harled structure with a crenellated parapet, was built by the eccentric 5th Laird of Pitfour, Admiral George Ferguson, who died in 1867. It was purchased and restored by Banff and Buchan District Council in 1993.

Inside the entrance, 17 wooden steps on the left lead to the first floor, but if you want to go higher take the metal stairs on the right – 49 steps – leading to the second floor. Here, a series of large windows open up an impressive panoramic view of Buchan. At each window, there is a description of what can be seen.

INFORMATION

Distance: 6km (4 miles) circular.

Start and finish: Picnic area near Fetterangus. To get there take the A90 Aberdeen–Fraserburgh road, past Ellon, and then the A952 to Mintlaw. Continue on A952 and about 3 km north of Mintlaw turn left to Fetterangus. There are signs pointing the way to the car park and picnic area near Pitfour Observatory.

Terrain: Good walking on roads and tracks. Some sections can be muddy. Strong footwear recommended.

Toilets: Fetterangus (all year) and White Cow woods (seasonal).

Refreshments: At Aden Country Park or in Mintlaw.

Public transport: None convenient. Car necessary.

Looking east from the Observatory

Admiral Ferguson, who became Laird of Pitfour in 1821, did his best to outdo his predecessors. The Admiral, who was the illegitimate son of George Ferguson, 4th Laird of Pitfour, was (perhaps surprisingly for a naval man) always happiest on the back of a horse. He built great stables north of Pitfour House (now demolished), and opened a riding school. Then, in 1845, he built his racecourse.

Looking north from the Observatory, following the line of the track to the car park, you can see in the distance the high ground where the Admiral built the racetrack. Our route to it is to go back down the entrance path and turn right onto the track from the car park. Go right again at the bottom of the slope, and then continue straight on, heading in a westerly direction. Pass a large field on your left and re-enter the wood.

Continue along the main track, ignoring all side tracks, as it swings round the forest. Reach a minor

The Pitfour Observatory

road at Auchmachar Lodge and turn right. There is a good view of the Observatory away to the right and Mormond Hill with its array of aerials ahead. You can also clearly see the White Horse at the west end of Mormond Hill. Reach the White Cow Woods car park. There is a good picnic site here, and optional forest trails if you wish to extend your walk.

There are also toilets here (open spring to autumn). To continue the walk, turn right, back into the forest. In 500m at a T-junction, turn right, walking along the edge of the forest. This track is part of the 7km racecourse the Admiral had built in 1845. Perhaps he wanted to watch the races from his Observatory?

The track curves left. At the second junction, turn right on a broad track between fields. It is more than likely that this was where the races started and finished, for it was well within sight of the Observatory, although the Admiral would have needed his telescope to see which horse was first past the post. The tower is about half a mile from the racecourse; why it was built so far away is anybody's guess. It may have been because it was nearer Pitfour House. After reaching buildings on the left, the track becomes surfaced and swings left at houses to return you to the car park where you started.

Just before reaching the car park, there is a gate across a track on your left. The 1870 map shows a circular area in the Den of Howie near the track marked "Shelters". What the shelters were seems to be a mystery. Shelters for the horses? Shelter for the laird and his guests? Who knows! At any rate, it is here that we take our leave of the Admiral, one of the most picturesque figures of the last century in Buchan, and of the corner of Buchan that became the Ascot of the North.

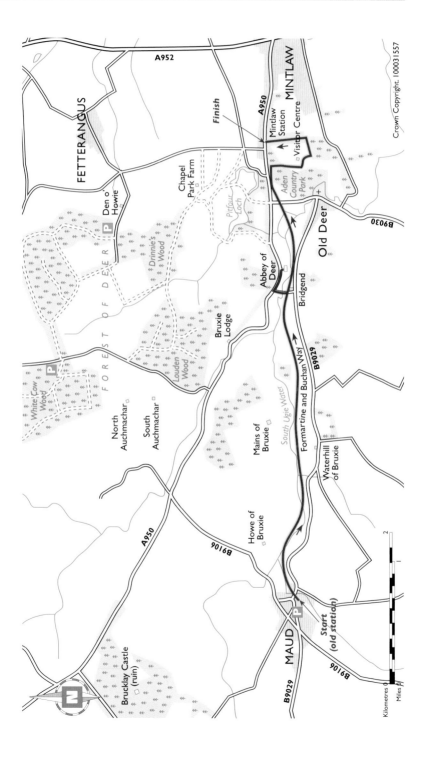

Crown Copyright. 100031557

MAUD TO ADEN

When the railway came to Buchan in 1866 the little village of Maud was suddenly put on the map. It became an important railway junction for lines branching north and east to Fraserburgh and Peterhead. It also helped the village to become a market centre for Buchan cattle. Today, by comparison, the mart has closed and the railway has gone. But you can still go down the Buchan line – on foot. Much of it is now a footpath and cycleway called the Formartine and Buchan Way. This walk takes you along a section of the old railway from Maud to Mintlaw, ending at Aden Country Park, which has been described as "a haven for people and wildlife".

The railway offices on the platform have been divided into work units for local businesses, while an attractive parking and picnic area has been laid out behind the station. One unit houses the Maud Railway Museum. There is also a well-preserved base of the old railway turntable located just beyond the end of the car park area, which will be of interest to railway enthusiasts.

From the station, follow one of the paths down to the Maud–Old Deer road (B9029). Cross the road and a little way down you will see a signposted ramp leading up to the Way. The path is narrow at the start, hemmed in by broom bushes, briar roses, bluebells, marguerites and other wild flowers. Yellow buttercups make a golden path of the old line. On this first stretch, it is hard to believe that

INFORMATION

Distance: 7km (4.5 miles) linear.

Start: Maud Station. From Aberdeen take the A90 to Ellon and follow the A948 north, branching off by the B9106 to Maud. Return from Aden to Maud by bus.

Terrain: Narrow footpath at start, widens to old railway track. No special footwear needed.

Toilets: At Aden Country Park.

Refreshments: Cafe/ restaurant at Aden Country Park.

Public transport: Stagecoach Bluebird, Service 251. For information, tel: 01224 212266.

Opening hours: *Aden Country Park:* All year round, daily, sunrise-sunset. *Heritage Centre,* May-Sept, daily 1000-1700. *Hareshowe Farm,* as Heritage Centre. *Wildlife Centre,* May-Sept, weekend only 1400-1700. *Maud Railway Museum:* weekends and public holidays from Easter to September, 1400-1630. *Abbey of Deer:* Open all year during daylight hours.

Old railway turntable at
Maud Station

trains once came puffing up the track. You cross a minor road going down to sewage works and then a rusty bridge spanning the South Ugie Water. There are occasional reminders of the railway days – numbered signs, a faded notice board at a farm crossing, a deserted linesman's hut.

Away on the right is Aikey Brae, once the setting for the biggest horse fair in the north-east of Scotland. But it has another claim to fame. It was here that the Battle of Aikey Brae was fought in 1308, when Edward Bruce, brother of Robert the Bruce, defeated the Comyn Earl of Buchan and wrought vengeance on the Comyn family with the herschip (harrying) of Buchan.

Less than a mile beyond Aikey Brae you can see on your left traffic on the road from New Pitsligo (A950) heading down past the Abbey of Deer on its way to Mintlaw. Road, river and rail track come together at Bridgend just before reaching the Abbey. There are actually two bridges here, a bridge over the railway track and the Abbey Bridge over the Ugie.

Abbey of Deer

The two-width Abbey Bridge

You can make a worthwhile diversion here to visit the Abbey of Deer. Leave the Way, go down onto the road at Bridgend and cross the Abbey Bridge. Reach the main road and turn right towards Mintlaw for a short (200m) walk to the Abbey entrance. Enter the Abbey grounds, which were the home of Cistercian monks from around 1219. The grounds are now cared for by Historic Scotland, and the remains are well laid out and interpreted to indicate the original use of the various buildings and rooms. Return to the old line to continue the walk.

Bridgend takes its name from the Abbey Bridge – and a very odd brig it is! Drivers crossing it find to their surprise that one half of the bridge is narrower than the other. The narrow half is on the south side of the bridge, the broad half on the north. The bridge marked the boundary between the estates of the Fergusons of Pitfour and the

Russells of Aden, and its present appearance stems from a feud between the two lairds. When the Fergusons built Pitfour Loch, the Russells said it would cause flooding in Aden. The Fergusons, however, went ahead with their loch-building, but the Laird of Aden got his revenge. When the Fergusons widened the bridge to allow coaches to pass over it, the Russells refused to widen their side. The result is a half-and-half bridge that should surely claim a place in the *Guinness Book of Records*.

The old Buchan line passes within a stone's throw of the Abbey walls, and a little farther on you can see Saplinbrae House, now a hotel, off the New Pitsligo-Mintlaw road. Incidentally, you can also see sticking up behind the hotel the top of the Pitfour Observatory, another of the mad Admiral's crazy creations (see Walk 16).

This stretch of the walk is a wilderness of wild flowers, trees and bushes closing in on you, while the road from Maud is on the right almost at your elbow. Then it's out into the open and across another iron bridge over the South Ugie. The South Lodge of Pitfour estate can be seen on the left and, after passing a stretch of aspen trees, you are almost at the path taking you into Aden Country Park.

Aden was home to generations of the Russell family. Now it draws visitors to Mintlaw. It boasts an award-winning Heritage Centre, where you can turn back the clock to life on the estate farm in the 1920s, and its restored farm buildings in the Round Square include a Horseman's House where bannocks and oatcakes are baked for visitors. There is also a working farm, an adventure playground, a cafe-restaurant, craftshop and much more.

The remains of Aden House

Having enjoyed the various attractions within the Park, you have the choice of catching a bus direct from outside the Park entrance back to Maud, or walking back along the track to return to Buchan's once great cattle town.

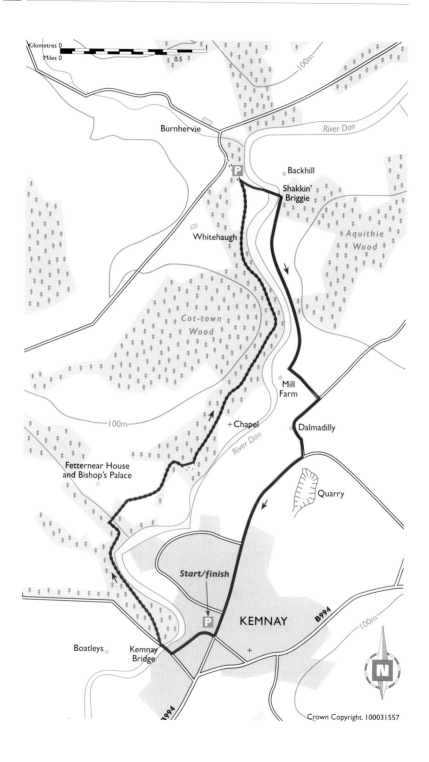

Kilometres 0

Miles 0 ———— 0.5

Burnhervie

River Don

Backhill

Shakkin'
Briggie

Whitehaugh

Aquithie
Wood

Cot-town
Wood

100m

Mill
Farm

+Chapel

Dalmadilly

River Don

Fetternear House
and Bishop's Palace

Quarry

Start/finish

KEMNAY

B994

100m

Boatleys

Kemnay
Bridge

N

B994

Crown Copyright. 100031557

FETTERNEAR

An ancient estate, where the Bishops of Aberdeen had a summer palace and a shooting lodge nearly eight centuries ago, is the setting for this walk. It follows a path along the banks of the River Don from Kemnay Bridge to the Shakkin' Briggie and Burnhervie, passing near to the ruins of a great mansion house.

From the car park in Kemnay, turn right along Aquithie Road, then right again at the first opening. This road takes you up and over the old railway line and down to Riverside Road where, taking another right-hand turn, you cross the Don by Kemnay Bridge. A short distance on is the entrance to the estate of Fetternear.

The imposing entrance gate carries a sign saying that pedestrians are welcome except when the gates are closed, which is rarely. There is, in fact, a small pedestrian gate set into the main gate, and the estate has no objection to this being used if the main gates are shut.

Beyond the gate, passing a lodge on the left, the track heads through the Fetternear woods, staying fairly close to the River Don at first. Across the river is a modern housing estate. Soon, track and river part company, the track bending away left.

INFORMATION

Distance: 9.5km (6 miles) circular.

Start and finish: Car park in Aquithie Road, Kemnay. From Aberdeen, take the A96 and branch left along the B994. Total distance is 22km (14 miles).

Terrain: Good paths all the way; no special footwear needed. If returning by road, there is a steep climb up from the Shakkin' Briggie to the road. Also, watch out for traffic on this route.

Toilets: In Kemnay.

Refreshments: In Kemnay.

Public Transport: Stagecoach Bluebird, West Gordon timetable, service 220 to Kemnay. Information, tel: 01224 212266.

The ruined House of Fetternear

Farther on, a rather dilapidated bridge crosses a burn on the right, taking you on the first leg of a track towards the Don. Looking across the fields on the left, you will see the ruins of the House of Fetternear, which succeeded the medieval Bishop's Palace. Practically nothing of the Palace remains.

The Palace, no longer being used as an episcopal residence, became uninhabitable in the middle of the 16th century, when the Barony came into the possession of the Leslies of Balquhain. William Leslie, 9th Baron Balquhain, built a new house, which was altered and improved by succeeding generations of Leslies. Over the years, it grew from a small tower house into a large mansion.

The end of the House of Fetternear came in December 1919 when a servant left a pan of hot ashes in a back store room which set fire to kindling, coals and oil. The mansion house was destroyed. Today, the house is a dangerous ruin, yet even seen from the distance its mellow sandstone walls retain some of its past glory.

Continuing on the walk, you come to a fork at a big old tree, where you should bear right, following the track on the line of the river. Across the Don is Kemnay Quarry, where silver-grey stone from the Hill of Paradise helped in the building of such national landmarks as the Holborn Viaduct in London, the Thames Embankment and the Forth Railway Bridge. Kemnay Academy can be seen near the quarry.

Going through a gate, you come to a large green corrugated barn which has seen better days. About 200 metres beyond the barn, before reaching a metal gate, a grassy path goes right towards the river and the Chapel Pot. A "pot" is a deep pool, and there are a number of pots on this stretch of the Don, among them Gilbert Pot and the Black Pot. North of the Chapel Pot, between Cottown Wood and Aquithie Wood (pronounced

Achweethie), the river runs in a picturesque "narrow" known as the Garples, where there is a Garples Pot.

The chapel path leads to the ruined river church of Fetternear, which stands beside an ancient walled kirkyard close to the river. The path branches off to the left

The old kirkyard by the river

and goes into a field, but your way lies straight ahead to a gate. Go through, turn left, and you are in the chapel grounds.

Rubble and stones lie all about you, and further into the grounds you come upon the stark remains of what was obviously a beautiful chapel. Two arched entrances can still be seen, and on the gable is a wall plaque with the initials IHS and IMJ and a cross above them.

It is a scene of total desolation. Curious oblong gravestones lie on the ground, their Latin inscriptions barely readable. One has the dates 1858-1870. Other stones lie flat on the ground, while upright gravestones, erected surprisingly close together, are almost buried in a wilderness of bracken. There is a sad, neglected look about the old kirkyard, almost as if Nature had been closing in on it, hiding it from prying eyes. The ruined chapel is a comparatively modern building, but it is said that there was a chapel on the site as far back as 1109. St Ninian's Well springs between the church and the river.

Retrace your steps to the main path and continue, passing a short stretch of dyke on the left which has two or three steps going up to a narrow path. Whatever its original function, it now leads nowhere, running out among the trees. On your right, the river ripples on its way, making a great curve to the north as it heads towards Inverurie,

Kintore and finally Aberdeen and the sea. There is a saying, "Ae rood o' Don's worth twa o' Dee" (a rood is 160th of a Scots acre) and the walk by the river at Fetternear may well persuade you that the old maxim is true. Keep an eye open for swans and herons on the river.

Stick to the right when you come to another fork. A sign, "Lower Hut", indicates a fishing bothy by the river. From here you get your first glimpse of the Shakkin' Briggie.

Continuing on the main path you go through a closed gate (shut it behind you) and in front is another entrance to the estate. Beyond it is Whitehaughs' Lodge, where there is a notice offering honey for sale. The honey is superb! Past the Lodge is a tarred road which turns down towards the river, passing Riverside Cottage. A stone bridge crosses a burn running into the Don and the remains of a mill lade can be seen.

Just ahead is a large open space where people going over the bridge can leave their cars. Walkers starting from the Burnhervie side of the estate also park their cars here. It is a long and impressive briggie – and it does shake! You would be well

The Shakkin' Briggie

advised to pay attention to the notice, "Do not swing on the bridge".

The road beyond Whitehaugh Lodge runs along a line of beech trees which must have marked a Lovers' Walk at one time – and maybe still does. At any rate, dozens of couples have carved their initials on the trees. One goes back to 1945 and there are probably older ones. It makes you wonder what romantic stories lie behind them. Who were JR and MB, or SB and MK? Will we ever know?

Burnhervie is a quiet little hamlet where roads go off to the Chapel of Garioch, Inverurie, Fetternear and Monymusk. The Don twists and turns on its way to Burnhervie, reminding us of another old saying: "He has as many crooks as the Don".

The last pot on this beautiful stretch of the river is at Burnhervie – Ree Pot. The word "ree" means a pen for cattle and sheep, and the Ree Pot is the pot beside the enclosure.

Burnhervie is the turning point of the walk, but you have the choice of retracing your steps along the river bank or crossing the Shakkin' Briggie and going back to Kemnay by road. Once over the bridge, there is a steep climb up a path to a lay-by which marks the end of the road.

Whether you arrange for a car to pick you up at the Shakkin' Briggie lay-by or go by foot, you set off high above the river, looking down the long sweep of the Don and across to the path that took you to the bridge.

If you are walking, watch out for traffic, for it is a narrow road and there are lots of bends. When you come to a T-junction, turn right, and right again at the next T-junction. You are now on the main road into Kemnay. There is a footpath on the right-hand side of the road, which passes Kemnay Quarry and takes you straight back to the car park.

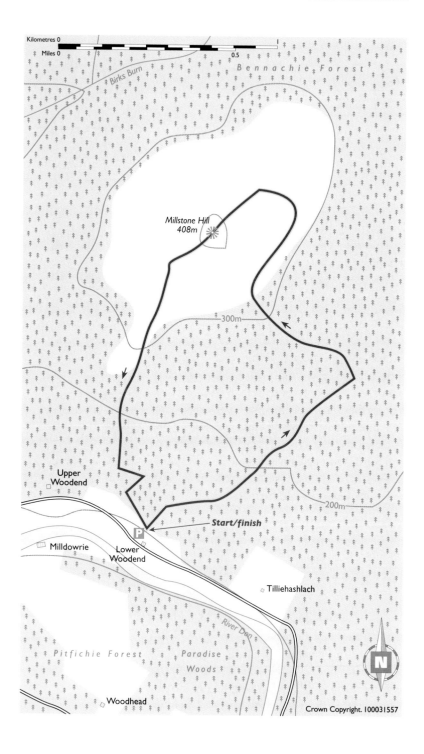

Kilometres 0   1
Miles 0   0.5

B e n n a c h i e   F o r e s t

Birks Burn

Millstone Hill
408m

300m

Upper
Woodend

200m

Start/finish

P

Milldowrie

Lower
Woodend

Tilliehashlach

River Don

P i t f i c h i e   F o r e s t

*Paradise
Woods*

N

Woodhead

Crown Copyright. 100031557

MILLSTONE HILL

Although the Mither Tap draws hundreds of people up the slopes of Bennachie, many walkers prefer to head for its "little sister" – Millstone Hill. Millstone is a spur of Bennachie, rising above the River Don, north of Monymusk, and offering a challenge a little less daunting than the bigger hill. Yet it gives an unsurpassed view of the Garioch countryside and of the Mither Tap itself.

The starting point is the Donview Centre, run by the Forestry Commission. The Centre itself is now closed to the public. Outside, there are car parking spaces and picnic tables, toilets, a map of the area, and directions on the routes to take.

After looking at the information board, take the right hand path behind the board, following the green arrow up a short tree-identification trail. The path climbs up and crosses a broad forest track to enter the wood on the other side. A steepish climb follows, but it is easily tackled if you are reasonably fit. Cross a second forest road and follow the green arrow into a cleared and replanted area which has abundant wild flowers in springtime. Leave this area by crossing a third forest road and re-entering the older trees, now following an orange arrow.

INFORMATION

Distance: 4km (2.5 miles) circular.

Start and finish: Donview Centre. To get to the Centre, take the A96 from Aberdeen, branching off on the B994 to Kemnay. From Kemnay, continue to Monymusk on the B993, turning right through the village. Cross the River Don, bearing left, and follow a signposted road to the Donview Centre (the Centre is now closed to the public, but the car park, toilets and walks are available).

Terrain: Woodland and hill tracks, some rough and narrow. Route down from Millstone Hill is steep and in wet weather can be slippery. Hill boots or strong shoes recommended. Also warm clothing – it can be cold at the top!

Toilets: At Donview Centre, closed November–March.

Refreshments: Nearest shops, cafes, at Monymusk and Kemnay.

The Mither Tap from Millstone Hill

Cairn William seen from
Millstone Hill

Eventually you will clear the woods for the last time. The path now narrows and skirts along the east shoulder of Millstone Hill. Soon the path turns uphill on a short sharp climb on pitched steps to a flat area from where you get your first view of the lumpy tor on the Mither Tap of Bennachie. Another familiar 'bump' can be seen behind you – the distant peak of Clachnaben.

There is a signpost at this fork pointing to Esson's car park and the Back of Bennachie. Esson's car park, just off the road from Monymusk to the Chapel of Garioch, boasts a magnificent new Bennachie Visitors' Centre. You can see it on the walk from the Rowan Tree car park (Walk 20).

Meantime, you are on the last lap of the climb to the rocky summit of Millstone Hill. It is a hard push, but well worth the effort, for there is no more impressive view of the Mither Tap than the one from here. Standing by the cairn on Millstone, Bennachie's great knotted head provides a breath-taking silhouette against the sky. It looks huge and formidable against little Millstone, but the Mither Tap is only 109m (358 ft) higher – 408m (1340 ft) compared with 517m (1698 ft).

Up there you are looking into Paradise – literally. Across the Don to the south are Paradise Woods, planted over two centuries ago by a famous "improver", Sir Archibald Grant of Monymusk. There is a narrow pass here called My Lord's Throat, named after Lord Forbes of Castle Forbes, and when visitors ask how they can get to Paradise they are told "Doon the Lord's Throat". "Doon the Lord's Throat, an' ootower Bennachie", wrote the Garioch poet Charles Murray. Well, we've been "ootower Bennachie" and now we are heading down Millstone towards the Lord's Throat.

From the top, go down the west side of the hill following the brown arrow on a good gravel path through scattered trees. On your left, the grey granite rock of Pitfichie Hill and Cairn William can be seen rising up behind Paradise Woods. Millstone Hill takes its name from mill stones of red granite which were at one time quarried on the hill.

As you go down the hill, you can see the Don winding its way through the Garioch towards Monymusk. You can actually pick out the main street of the village. The bridge over the Don at Pitfichie is just discernible without binoculars, and to the right of it is Pitfichie Castle.

Straight ahead, you get a lovely glimpse of the distant Don framed in the trees. Lower down, the path becomes steep and rocky, and care is required here. Eventually, you enter the dark forest down sleeper steps, at the foot of which you should follow the arrows as the path zigzags its way back to the car park. At the end of the walk, doubtless you will be a convert to Bennachie's "sister" hill.

Looking towards the Don from Millstone Hill

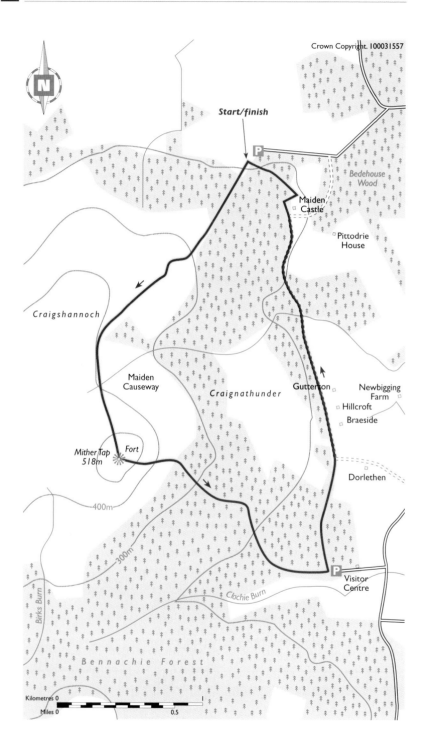

Start/finish

Bedehouse Wood

Maiden Castle

Pittodrie House

Craigshannoch

Maiden Causeway

Craignathunder

Gutterton

Newbigging Farm

Hillcroft

Braeside

Mither Tap 518m   Fort

Dorlethen

400m

300m

Visitor Centre

Birks Burn

Clachie Burn

Bennachie Forest

Kilometres 0   1
Miles 0   0.5

OVER AND UNDER THE MITHER TAP

Pick a dry, clear day for this walk as the Mither Tap is quite exposed, but offers excellent views over much of north-east Scotland.

The Rowan Tree car park is attractively laid out with toilets, picnic tables above the parking area, a map of Bennachie and its seven peaks, and an information board about the Mither Tap. The Maiden Causeway runs from the car park to the summit. Its origins are unknown, although one fanciful tale says that a local laird imprisoned and raped maidens in the fort on the top of the hill. On the other hand, some maps show a Maiden Castle at the foot of the hill.

Walk up the Maiden Causeway, a long steady pull-up, watching out for Hosie's Well on the right of the path. The story goes that a local man found that his sweetheart had married another while he was a captive after the battle of Harlaw in 1411. It is said that the water in the well is his tears. At the top of the Causeway, go through the gap in the wall of the fort and climb up to the indicator on the hilltop. Look out for the "thieves' mark" on the summit, a square cut in the rock with the initials P, LE, B (referring to estate names) and the date 1858.

Great care should be taken here, but take your time and enjoy the view to the full.

INFORMATION

Distance: 9km (5.5 miles) circular.

Start and finish: Rowan Tree car park. Take the A96 Aberdeen-Inverness road, branching off beyond Inverurie on the road to Chapel of Garioch. Continue through Chapel of Garioch until you come to a sign pointing left on the road to the Rowan Tree car park.

Terrain: Track clear all the way, but surface rough in places.

Toilets: Rowan Tree car park and Esson's car park.

Transport: Car necessary.

Worth seeing: Pictish hill fort and Bennachie Visitor Centre.

Opening hours: Bennachie Centre: open Tue-Sun, late March-late October 1030-1700, Nov-late March 0930-1600 Closed every Monday.

Bennachie Visitor Centre

Climb down and back out of the fort entrance and spot a green post indicating the route to Bennachie Centre. Follow the orange arrows down through the woods to the Centre, watching out for one or two ruins on the way which were part of the Colony. The Colony began with a handful of squatters, but by 1859 there were nearly 60 crofters living in 12 homesteads on the hill. They were harried by local lairds who wanted to divide the hill between themselves. One by one they left the area until finally only one remained – John Esson, whose son George lived there until 1939. Hence the name Esson's car park, beside the Centre.

After visiting the Centre, take the gravel path from the information board to the right, going behind the Centre. Pass a strange bird carving on your left, and where the gravel path bends sharply left, go straight ahead with a young coniferous plantation on your right. The path narrows through birch and rowan till it reaches the road to Dorlethen, where it widens.

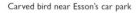
Carved bird near Esson's car park

There is a sinister story about Dorlethen. In a letter written in 1938, George Esson, who was a crofter on Bennachie for nearly 50 years, mentioned the death of the Dorlethen farmer, a man called Hay. "There was a very mysterious occurrence about a child of his stepdaughter," he wrote. "It was lost. It disappeared away from Dorlethen and its body was found on the Hill when they were cutting trees 7 years afterwards at the head of the Boddach road. It was just 22 months old and it could not manage to climb up there by itself, I don't think. There was a

Public Inquiry in Aberdeen but nothing was decided about it as there was no evidence". Dorlethen looks innocent enough today.

Keep straight on, passing Braeside, and the two white houses of Hillcroft and Gutterton with Newbigging farm behind. At a fork keep right, going downhill, then up, ignoring a track on the left. At this point – about half way between the Rowan Tree car park and Esson's – a crag on Bennachie, which rises on your left, is shown on maps as Craignathunder, pronounced Craignathunner. This has been dismissed as a distortion of an old name, but James Macdonald, a well-known place-name expert a century ago, thought that "thunder" was a corruption of a Gaelic hill-name, *Ton re gaoith*, meaning "backside to the wind".

Look out for Pittodrie House Hotel nestling in the trees across a field. It is an interesting building dating back to the early 17th century. The wood on the left is known as Bedehouse Wood, and somewhere among the trees are the remains of a Bede House (almshouse). It stood by the Linn Burn near Pittodrie House, and there is an interesting tale attached to it. In the time of King Charles II it was built by William Erskine of Pittodrie for four poor men. It consisted of "two chambers and one midroom". The four men were each given one peck of meal and half a peck of malt each week, but they had to wear livery gowns and go to church on Sundays.

Pass the back gate to Pittodrie House on the right, with the kennels cottage just inside the gate. Turn left up the hill and in fifty metres take the right hand path through the woods till you reach the outer route on the Maiden's Causeway. Turn right here and go down the last 300 metres to the Rowan Tree and the car.

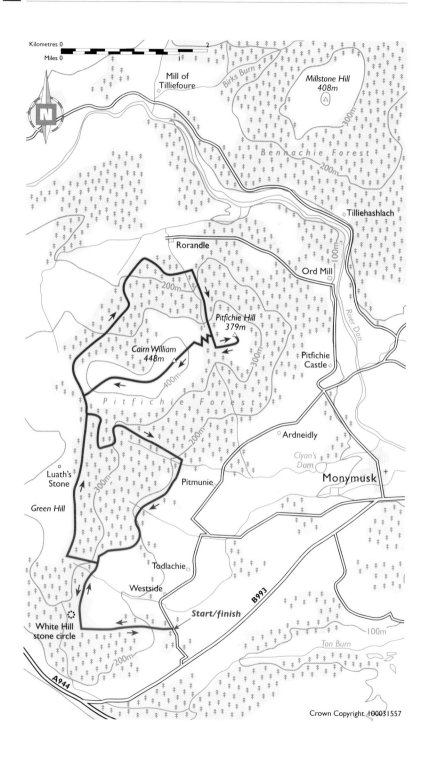

Kilometres 0 | 2
Miles 0 | 1

N

Mill of Tilliefoure

Birks Burn

Millstone Hill 408m

Bennachie Forest

300m

200m

Tilliehashlach

Rorandie

1000m

Ord Mill

200m

Pitfichie Hill 379m

River Don

Cairn William 448m

300m

Pitfichie Castle

400m

Pitfichie Forest

Ardneidly

200m

Clyan's Dam

Monymusk

Luath's Stone

300m

Pitmunie

Green Hill

200m

Todlachie

Westside

B993

Start/finish

White Hill stone circle

100m

Ton Burn

200m

A944

Crown Copyright. 100031557

CAIRN WILLIAM AND PITFICHIE

This is a forest and hill walk. Alternative routes can be taken to cut out some of the hilltops, but this would mean missing the superb views from the Cairn William ridge and Pitfichie Hill. After studying the information board at the parking area, go round the gate and head uphill on the forest track until you reach a green post. Here, turn right and soon a tall standing stone on the left marks the site of the White Hill Stone Circle, which dates back to the Bronze Age. Apparently this was once one of the best of its kind in the district, but neglect and vandalism have taken their toll, and most of the stones are lying in the heather and bracken.

Leaving this tranquil spot, carry on along the forest track to a green post with a red arrow. Go left (uphill) on a narrow path through mixed larch and pine to reach the open top of Green Hill, with fine views westward to the Vale of Alford. As you drop down the far side of the hill, a large solitary standing stone can be seen on your left near some small trees. This is Luath's Stone, traditionally associated with a son of Macbeth, King of Scotland in the 11th century. It seems more likely that the stone was erected long before Luath's time, and the name may simply mean grey stone –

INFORMATION

Distance: 13km (8 miles) circular.

Start and finish: Pitfichie Forest. Take the A944 Aberdeen–Alford road for about 30km (18 miles), then branch right on the B993 Inverurie road. Soon go left at a sign for Pitfichie Forest Cycle Trails. In about 800m, go left up a forest track to the parking area.

Terrain: Clear tracks and paths all the way, but strong footwear and warm clothing recommended as paths are rough and muddy in places and the hilltops can be breezy. Alternative routes are available.

Toilets and refreshments: None on route. Nearest in Alford, 9km (5.5 miles).

Transport: Car necessary.

White Hill stone circle site

"liath" in Gaelic. As the heather is very deep and rough, it is difficult to get to the stone, but it stands an impressive 3m tall with a girth at the base of 2.9m.

Carry on downhill, heading towards the long ridge of Cairn William ahead. When you reach a forest track at a turning circle, turn left along the track and follow it by the blue arrows, ignoring a red arrow going right – this is your return route. The shapely cones of Ben Rinnes and Tap o' Noth are prominent to the north-west. At the end of the forest track, go in the direction of the blue arrow on a path into the forest, and eventually downhill to a main forest track.

As you descend, you get your first glimpse of the Mither Tap of Bennachie ahead. Before turning right on the forest track, look straight ahead through the trees and you will see Cornabo Farm, the buildings of which have been converted into private houses. Legend has it that King Robert the Bruce once stayed at Cornabo.

Carry on along the forest track and soon you will see a bigger farm below to your left. This is Rorandle, which originally had a coach house which was a stopping point for drovers as they herded their cattle over the drove road from Monymusk to Alford. The Rorandle farmer has called the view over his farm to Bennachie 'the million dollar view' – it is certainly very impressive.

The next green post on the track has a red arrow pointing uphill, and this is the start of your return route, climbing fairly steeply up a path bordered on the upper stretch by an attractive old, mossy stone dyke. When you reach level ground, at a post with a red arrow, you have three choices. To avoid the higher hilltops, go straight ahead to a T-junction, turn right and return to the car park on the forest track. To climb Pitfichie Hill, go ahead for 200m to a green post with red arrows pointing

Ancient stones on White Hill

uphill to the left. To climb Cairn William, turn right and zigzag through a young wood to the open hill and a pull up to the trig point.

After enjoying beautiful views, walk along the fairly level ridge for about 1.5km. On your right, Castle Forbes may be seen among its trees, and away to the left you might be able to pick out Luath's Stone, passed earlier on the walk. The path drops down to rejoin the main forest track on the outward route. Turn left and follow the blue arrows all the way down, turning right at a post with a car park sign which directs you back to the start of the walk.

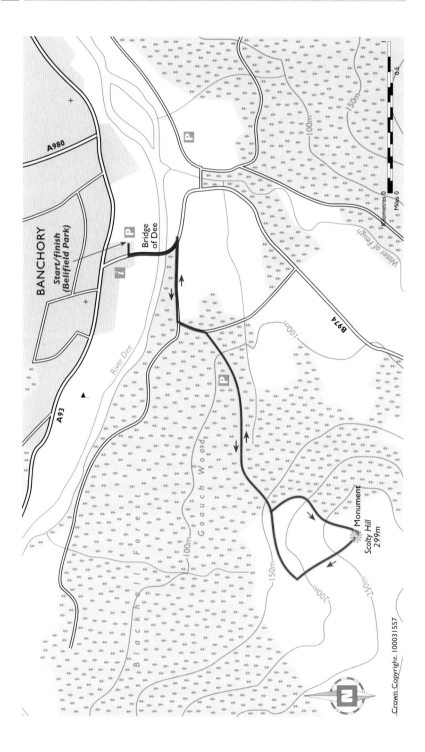

Crown Copyright. 100031557

SCOLTY HILL

Scolty Hill, on the outskirts of Banchory, might have remained a small and undistinguished peak if someone hadn't put a tower on top of it. That was in 1842, when the tower was erected in memory of General William Burnett of Banchory Lodge. Since then, Scolty's Tower has been a familiar landmark on Lower Deeside.

It has also been a favourite walk for both locals and visitors. To get there, walk down Banchory's Dee Street and cross the Bridge of Dee, bearing left on the A943, then turn sharp right up the Auchattie road. You can cut the corner by climbing a stepped path opposite the south end of the bridge. About 500m up the Auchattie road, turn left at the junction signposted Scolty Hill and look for a rough road branching off to the right about 150m ahead.

Follow this road uphill as far as cars can go; there is ample parking here. A network of paths has been established within the Scolty Woodland, part of the Forestry Commission's Blackhall Forest. There is an information board with a clearly marked choice of low-level walks, but for the route to the top of Scolty, follow the waymarked white arrows directly ahead until a wooden gate bars the way.

INFORMATION

Distance: 8 km (5 miles) circular, with 220m ascent.

Start and finish: Bridge Street, Banchory. See text for details of approach to Scolty.

Terrain: Mostly good track, rougher on final climb to the summit. Boots or strong shoes recommended.

Refreshments: Wide choice in Banchory.

Toilets: In Banchory.

Information: Tourist information centre in the car park at Bridge Street.

Woodland Park signboard

Scolty Tower

Once through the gate, go left for 150m, keeping your eye open for a footpath on the right. This leads up the hill through open woodlands of birch, interspersed with Scots pine, with the fenced-in Forestry Commission plantation on the left. The track gets steeper and stonier the higher you climb. Finally, the tower is seen over the brow of the hill, the trees are left behind, and you are up on the bare plateau.

The tower is built on a large circular area of ground, with two indicators picking out the distant hills – Peter Hill in the Forest of Birse; the familiar lump of Clachnaben; Clachan Yell, rising above Glen Tanar; Mount Keen, the most easterly Munro; and a handful of lesser peaks. The indicator on the other side points to Morven, Mortlich and even the humble Tyrebagger near Aberdeen.

Banchory lies below, stretching out from the winding Dee. This Deeside town, which has become almost a dormitory for Aberdeen, must have been a good deal smaller and less lively when the tower was erected in 1842 by General Burnett's "numerous friends and tenantry". He died three years earlier, in 1839, at the age of 72. He was a veteran of the Napoleonic Wars. Not much has been written about him, but he was said to be "a public spirited gentleman and a kind landlord, whose memory will be long and gratefully cherished in this neighbourhood."

The extensive view from Scolty Hill

Now that the staircase inside the tower has been renewed, visitors can climb up the metal steps and get an even loftier bird's-eye view of the surrounding countryside. The Prince of Wales came along to have a look at it. There is a plaque on the tower commemorating his visit on 15 September 1992, "on the occasion of the 150th anniversary and the restoration of the monument by the Rotary Club of Banchory Ternan."

Scolty Tower looks down on the vast expanse of Blackhall Forest. Blackhall, which today covers some 1200 hectares, once boasted a castle – Blackhall Castle, originally the seat of the Bannerman family. It was in fact, a pseudo-castle, a mansion house built in the castellated style, and was eventually demolished. From Scolty you can see the Invercannie waterworks, which supplies Aberdeen with its water. In the days when timber was brought down the Dee in log-rafts, one of the most difficult parts of the journey was the "Glisters", on the Blackhall Castle stretch opposite the waterworks.

The woods around Scolty were planted in 1941 to replace large-scale felling by Canadian lumberjacks during the last war. Although Blackhall is Forestry Commission property, the top of Scolty is owned by a local farmer. This comes about because the bare ground around the summit forms part of the farmlands of Ardlair, which lies south of the hill.

Paths can be seen running across the neighbouring slopes towards the oddly-named Hill of Goauch and on to the Shooting Greens on the west side of the forest, but these should be left to hill-walkers and runners who know the area. There are other paths in Blackhall that can be explored, but the only one of consequence to Scolty walkers, apart from the climb up the hill, is one which drops down the west side and circles round it to join the main path at the wooden gate. From there it is a straight walk back to the car.

The return route opens up a striking view of the country to the north of the River Dee, and particularly the long ridge of the Hill of Fare.

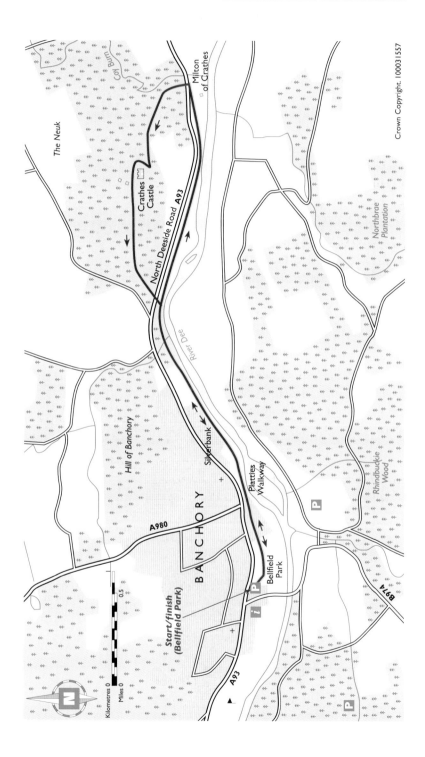

BANCHORY TO CRATHES

"A pearl of great price among the nation's jewels" — that's how Crathes Castle was once described by the historian Dr W. Douglas Simpson. This walk takes you to Crathes by the old Deeside railway line, where once the lairds of Crathes had their own personal Halt. There is an ambitious plan to restore the railway as a tourist attraction between Banchory and Crathes, but a parallel path for walkers is guaranteed as part of the project.

From the Dee Street car park in Banchory, take a tarmac path going east through Bellfield Park, with the North Deeside Road (A93) on your left and the River Dee on your right. After passing under an old railway bridge, go right by a footpath which skirts a small housing estate built on the site of Banchory railway station.

Continue along the path until you come to the old engine sheds. The station was built on the site of the original village of Banchory. One Deeside author, James Coutts, didn't think much of it. In his *Dictionary of Deeside* in 1899, he said it was "neither well built nor well situated, being placed at the eastern outskirts close to the churchyard, as if designed for nearness to the dead rather than the living."

The gateway into the kirkyard is on your left and when you go through it you will see a building erected when other people were showing a gruesome

INFORMATION

Distance: 9.5 km (5.5 miles) circular.

Start and finish: Dee Street car park, Banchory. Banchory is 30 km (18 miles) west of Aberdeen on A93.

Terrain: Paths in park, then old railway track to Crathes Castle. Take care if including Platties Walkway on the return journey.

Toilets: In Banchory Castle and at Crathes Castle.

Refreshments: Café at Crathes Castle and Milton Restaurant, adjacent to the castle, as well as an abundance of eating places in Banchory.

Public transport: Good bus service from Aberdeen to Banchory and Crathes. Stagecoach Bluebird Coach, service 201; information: (01224) 212266.

Opening hours: *Crathes Castle*: 1 Apr.–end Oct., 1000–1730 daily. Last admission 1645 (admission charge). Garden and grounds open all year daily, 0930 to sunset.

Part of the walled garden at Crathes Castle

interest in the dead. This is an unusual two-storeyed circular mort-house used as a Watch Tower when body-snatchers were on the prowl.

Take the wide track to the left of the Watch Tower, and when you come to the end of a low wall on your right, turn right to rejoin the track.

The waste-water treatment works and the Silverbank sawmills are on your left; on the right you come to an open space where anglers may be seen. Where a gated track goes up to the sawmills, the railway track does a small twist and continues on its way, but look for another path going into the woods directly in front of you. It runs parallel with the main track, but it is closer to the river and gives you pleasant views of the Dee.

Further on, a bridge spans a burn running into the Dee and some rough steps take you up the embankment to the railway line. Beyond the bridge another path takes you back to the riverbank. There are stepping stones over the burn, but when the stream is swollen by rain a crossing here is not advised. Soon you will see a fishing bothy ahead; this is where you turn up to the old railway line. Before the bothy go up the embankment, through a small gate, and onto the main track.

Just above you is a stretch of the old North Deeside Road, and a lay-by where second-hand sleepers for the proposed rail track are stored. Keep heading along the old line for 1.5km, close to the main road. The bridge at Crathes, and the masts on Cairn mon Earn, can be seen in the distance.

At Milton of Crathes you reach a large car park for the small businesses housed in the original cottages and steadings, but also a display of railway carriages and a short stretch of relaid rail track, the opening stage of the proposed Banchory to Crathes rail link.

At this point, follow the footpath between the cottages to a small tarmac track beside the Coy Burn, which goes past St Ternan's football field on the right. Just before this track cuts through the old rail embankment, look out for a small path on your right which leads – it's only about 20 metres – to the historic packhorse bridge over the Coy Burn.

Return to the track which goes under a bridge on the A93, taking you on to the main avenue into the estate of Crathes Castle, one of the finest in the northeast, and now in the care of the National Trust for Scotland. There is a footpath to the left of the avenue, waymarked with white arrows. The route to the castle passes a lovely lochan on the right, and at one point the waymarked path crosses the road into a wood, to emerge just below the castle car park.

Crathes Castle

Your way back is via the West Gate. Follow the tarmac path downhill with the castle on your left. Shortly afterwards, take the right fork, which may have a light chain across to deter vehicles. Thereafter, ignore paths going left or right; stick to the main route to the West Gate, passing Caroline's Garden.

When you reach the West Gate turn left onto the North Deeside Road, cross the road to the other side and watch for a path going down into the old lay-by. From here another path takes you onto the Deeside line. Return by the railway track to the east side of Banchory until you come to the riverbank beside the kirkyard. Here look out for a sign on your left to the Platties Walkway by the edge of the river.

The Platties takes its name from the concrete platforms used in its construction. Early last century, when the station underwent substantial rebuilding, the project included the construction alongside the River Dee of a massive retaining wall with a right of way at its foot known as the Platties. There is a fine view up the river, where the Feugh comes tumbling in to join it, and in the distance you can see the familiar tower on Scolty Hill (Walk 22).

From the Platties, it is an easy walk back to Bellfield Park and your car.

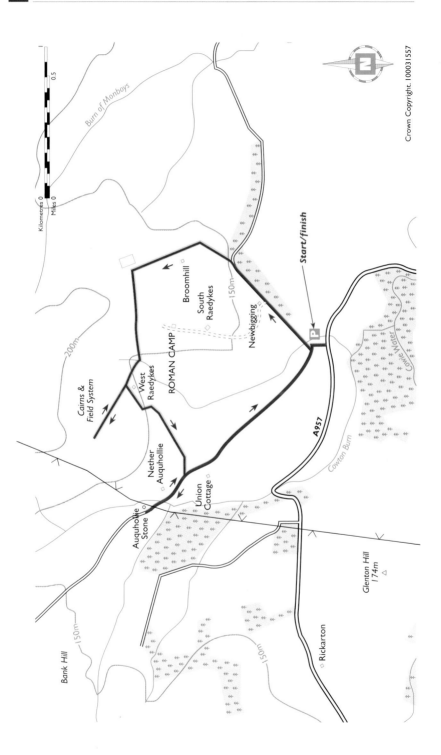

Crown Copyright. 100031557

Burn of Monboys

Kilometres 0   0.5
Miles 0

200m

Cairns &
Field System

West
Raedykes

ROMAN CAMP

Nether
Auquhollie

Auquhollie
Stone

Union
Cottage

Bank Hill
150m

Broomhill

South
Raedykes

Newbigging

150m

Start/finish

P

A957

Cowton Burn

Colne Water

Glenton Hill
174m

Rickarton

RAEDYKES AND CAMPSTONE HILL

This walk is a rewarding trip – first back to Roman Scotland, and then even further back to the Bronze Age, to see the ring cairns on Campstone Hill. Bring a vivid imagination under your woolly hat for this exploration back in time. Or just enjoy the grand views of the coast around Stonehaven and of the rolling hills to the south.

From the lay-by, at the fork ahead take the road signposted right to Netherley. Follow the lane uphill past South Raedykes Farm to your left. After half a mile, at the point the road turns to the right, go straight ahead on the track as far as Broomhill Farm. Here you can look east across moorland to the sea, with glimpses of the coastal towns of Stonehaven, and Newtonhill further north.

Instead of turning left into the farmyard, enter the field and discover the edge of the Roman marching camp of Raedykes. The experts are unsure when this substantial camp was built; no coins have been found on the site to suggest a date. But it is thought possible that the famous battle of Mons Graupius may have taken place near Stonehaven. Whatever the truth, strategically the Romans made a canny choice here of a sloping site, which guarded the route north to the Dee, as

INFORMATION

Distance: 8km (5 miles) circular. Excluding Auquhollie Stone, 6km (3.5 miles).

Start and finish: Just off the A957 Stonehaven to Crathes road. Take the A957 (Slug Road) out of Stonehaven, past Mackie Academy. After 5km, you cross the bridge over Cowie Water. After a further 500m, take a right turn signposted to Netherley. Almost immediately, look for a small lay-by under trees, suitable for parking a few cars.

Terrain: Quiet road and good tracks to and from farms. No marked footpath off track. Strong footwear recommended.

Transport: Access by car is recommended.

Refreshments and toilets: None on route. Nearest in Stonehaven.

Further reading: *Highways and Byways Round Stonehaven*, by Archibald Watt (Stonehaven Heritage Society, 1992).

Bronze Age cairns on Campstone Hill

well as overlooking the coast and approaches from the south.

What remains are parts of the characteristic fortifications built to protect the troops from hostile Caledonians. Ahead of you is a clear ditch – or *fossa* – with its turf rampart, on which would once have been a wooden palisade. Trace the line of the *fossa* as far as the farm fence, then turn left following the line of the fence uphill round a corner to the top of the field. In front of you is another long dramatic section of rampart, strongly built against possible invasion from higher ground to the north.

This large camp comprised as much as 38ha (93 acres) all round Garrison Hill to the west of Broomhill Farm, and may have temporarily housed as many as 15,000 men. Much of the original earthworks still exist and enthusiasts could happily explore for some time.

The Roman fossa at Raedykes

For a dramatic change of historical perspective, head for Campstone Hill. Follow the northern rampart, heading south-west to a junction of farm dykes. Cross to the north side of the *fossa* through a gate, and walk downhill towards the farm of West Raedykes, using field tracks and gates where possible.

At the farm, follow the track to the right, through a gate, and up the slope to your left. There is no discernible path, so make your own way up to the broad ridge of Campstone Hill. Here, a cairnfield remains from a Bronze Age settlement of Beaker people over 3,000 years ago. No one is quite sure whether all the numerous cairns indicate a cemetery, or if some of the piles of stones were cleared to mark boundaries.

But the real objective is four ring cairns, two of which are surrounded by striking circles of standing stones. These were certainly burial sites, in which the cremated remains were buried inside pottery urns covered by a dome of small stones. A prominent circle of larger stones guides you to the first ring cairn. Further on, two more exist, but are obscured by encroaching gorse. The fourth, at the top of the hill, includes some of the largest upright stones of the group and may have been the burial place of a chieftain.

Enjoy the views to Fetteresso to the south and Durris to the west, before retracing your steps to West Raedykes Farm. Take the farm track to its end. At this point, you can return to the start by turning left for less than 800m.

For the longer walk, turn right to see the Auquhollie Standing Stone. Walk along the road for about 1.2km, over the Cowton Burn and past Nether Auquhollie Farm, and this 2.3m high rock is prominent beside the next farm track on your right.

This impressive and solitary block of granite, which may once have formed part of a stone circle, is particularly interesting, not just because over the centuries it has avoided the fate of being used as a lintel above a fireplace or as part of a bothy wall, but because it is one of only 14 "ogham" inscribed stones found in Scotland. Ogham was an Irish form of alphabet used by the Gaelic-speaking Celts some time after the Romans withdrew from the area.

Auquhollie Standing Stone

On its south-east side is a clear ogham in-scription carved in short straight lines which is apparently a dedication to: "Avua Anunao soothsayer of Dovenio'". Who-ever he was, he must have merited a fine headstone. This, with a Pictish symbol on another face of the stone, dates it to a pe-riod around 400 AD, after the Romans but before Christian times in the area.

To return to the start, retrace your steps back down the lane, a distance of about 2km.

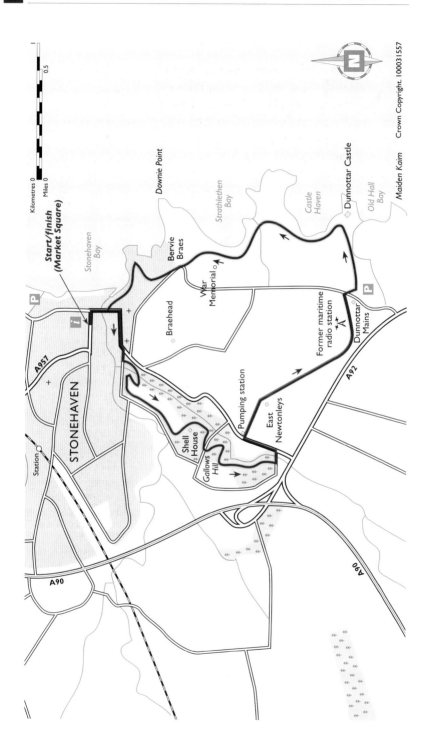

Start/finish
(Market Square)

Stonehaven Bay

Downie Point

Strathlethen Bay

Bervie Braes

War Memorial

Braehead

Castle Haven

Dunnottar Castle

Old Hall Bay

Maiden Kaim

Former maritime radio station

Dunnottar Mains

Pumping station

East Newtonleys

Shell House

Gallows Hill

STONEHAVEN

Station

A957

A90

A92

A90

Kilometres 0   1
Miles 0   0.5

Crown Copyright. 100031557

DUNNOTTAR WOODS AND CASTLE

Recent path developments around Stonehaven mean that an enjoyable and varied walk can be followed linking the town, woodland and the magnificent Dunnottar Castle, with a return along the cliff top. From the Market Square, head east into Allardice Street. Turn right and follow the road south, then west as it passes the police station and courthouse. When the main road turns sharp left, leave it and continue westwards towards Low Wood Road. There are signposts left for Dunnottar Woods.

Take the first path leading up through the narrow strip of woodland on the steep slope at the end of Carron Gardens. Bear right at the top of the slope and follow the edge of the field. Your route takes you anti-clockwise around the edge of this level field. Eventually pass an old quarry (now mainly filled in and grassed over) and join a wider track. At a crossroads on the track, go straight on, following a waymarked route to the Shell House. This path follows the northern section of a high stone and brick wall around a large walled garden, which once formed part of the grounds of Dunnottar House, now totally demolished. Visit the interesting Shell House, a small stone built structure decorated inside with many small and coloured shells, where your torch will

INFORMATION

Distance: 8km (5 miles) circular.

Start and finish: Market Square, Stonehaven. From Aberdeen take the A90 south to Stonehaven and leave the by-pass to enter the town. Market Square is in the centre of town off Allardice Street (turn right at the traffic lights).

Terrain: Streets, woodland and cliff paths. Strong footwear recommended, as is a small hand torch to view the interior of the Shell House and the Ice House.

Refreshments: Good choice in Stonehaven.

Toilets: In Stonehaven and at Dunnottar Castle (admission charge).

Public transport: Stagecoach Bluebird Services 106, 107 and 117 from Aberdeen to Stonehaven.

The Shell House

help to see the shells. A board nearby gives some details of the structure. It is thought the little house was built around 1810, probably as somewhere for Lady Kennedy's ten children to play.

The Ice House below Gallows Hill

Continue along the path past the Shell House, following along the burn, then climb up to meet a minor road. Turn right here and pass the entrance to Dunnottar Nursery, which operates from within the walled garden area. Continue for about 150m past the Nursery entrance and then turn left at the waymarked path towards Gallows Hill. First come to the Ice House, a bottle-shaped pit about 6m in depth. It is built of local sandstone and covered with a metal grille. It may be lit with power from the adjacent solar panel, but your torch will be useful if the interior is dark. This Ice House would have been used by Dunnottar House to store ice and game at a suitable temperature through the summer months.

Continue to the top of Gallows Hill, where executions were carried out until about 1850. The Gallows Hill is itself an ancient burial cairn, which was probably used about 4,000 to 5,000 years ago.

Now, retrace your steps back down to the road and turn right, back the way you came. Continue until opposite the Nursery entrance, then turn right along a path which skirts Gallows Hill. Along this path, beyond Gallows Hill, there is a turning left, down to the burn, where Lady Kennedy's Bath is located. This again is thought to have been built for the children to play in. It is stone-built in an oval shape, with sluices to control the level of the water.

Return to the main track and continue southwards to reach the picnic area at the southern end of the woodland. Leave the picnic area car park and turn left onto the A957 for a short distance before taking the next road on the right, where a round-roofed building stands on the corner (this is a Scottish Water pumping station).

Follow the road over the hill and past the former Maritime Radio station to a junction nearly opposite the car park for Dunnottar Castle. Turn right, then left, to reach the track down to the castle. The magnificent fortress is certainly worth a visit; allow at least two hours if you do wish to go inside the grounds. Dra-

Dunnottar Castle – a hugely impressive fortress

matically perched on its promontory, it appears impregnable and, indeed, the gatehouse was said to be the strongest in Scotland.

The castle resisted a siege by Cromwell's forces in 1652, during the course of which the minister's wife from Kinneff smuggled the Scottish crown regalia out of the castle in a laundry basket. Dunnottar Castle has been used a number of times for filming, including scenes from Zeffirelli's version of *Hamlet*. In summer the castle is open every day, but in winter it is closed Tuesday to Thursday.

Take the path that leads along the cliff and walk north, back towards Stonehaven. The path is clear, but as always with a cliff walk, due care is needed, especially with children.

The path rounds Castle Haven and Strathlethen Bay, with lots of birdlife evident, before heading inland past the imposing War Memorial, which is worth visiting. The path then meets the road at the top of Bervie Braes. Follow the road a short distance before turning right down a path leading towards the harbour area. Go round the harbour to the Tolbooth where an interesting museum can be visited during the summer months. Behind the Tolbooth is a new boardwalk path, "the Backies" which leads around the bay until a sign on the left points to the Market Square and the end of the walk.

INDEX